Heroic Eschatology

Restoring hope and optimism by killing the sacred cows of trending end-times beliefs

A Unique View of the Book of Revelation

BRIAN NICKENS
heroiceschatology.com

Acknowledgments

Special thanks to Gary and April Wenzel. Your friendship and support is humbling. I want to express the gratitude and love Doreen and I have for you both. May the fruit from this book become jewels on your crown.

I also want to thank Bill Johnson, Kevin Dedmon, and the ever-amazing Chris Overstreet. Your friendship and encouragement has helped to sustain my passion for God's Kingdom. Your prophetic words to me have been literal stepping stones toward destiny.

Doreen, you are the love of my life, and you're brilliant! Thanks for all those deep discussions that served as checks and balances along the way. I know my never-ceasing thoughts and ideas can get tiring, but you so graciously let me ramble and always gently kept my heart in check.

And special thanks to my children and grandchildren. Austin, Tara, Addyson, and Avery, you are such fun to hang out with. The two months we all spent in Costa Rica was bliss. That was the turning point of what has now become normal Christianity for our entire family. The healing miracles we all participated in proved to me that the very same power that raised Jesus from the dead resides in us all. Regardless of age or Christian maturity. When the prayer of a six year old (Addyson) became the final act of obedience and faith that delivered a grown man from imminent death of cancer to a complete healing and the salvation of an entire family, I think we all realized the simplicity of God's love and power in a way we had not known. Avery, you are a real trooper and your passion is infectious. I love the way you love.

Kristen and Brandon, Josie, Cru, and Sid. All I can say is, world! Look out! Here come the Buchanan's. Each one of you are so uniquely gifted and powerful. I couldn't help but think of Cru and Sid when I wrote the introduction to this book, "Raising Alexander." Josie, you're the best. God's favor is all over you. I don't know if I've ever seen such strength in so sweet a package.

Brandon and Kristen, Austin and Tara, you are beautiful! You are great parents and great spouses. The way you honor and look after each other is admirable. Doreen and I are so blessed to have such a great family.

Thank You, Jesus, for coming to me and calling me Your friend. Thank You, Holy Spirit, for filling me with such great joy. You never cease to surprise me with another facet of Yourself. Don't ever let me settle into stale religion, please! Thank You, God the Father, for calling me son. I am sorry it took me so long to get to know You. I want to be like You.

DEDICATION

I dedicate this book to my mother and father, Max and Margaret Nickens. The story of your lives is incredible. I am humbled by the hardships you endured so I could grow up in relative ease and security. I recently watched the classic movie Grapes of Wrath and couldn't help but think of your journey. From the farm fields of the south and Midwestern United States to the high desert of Idaho and on into suburbs of Southern California, your life story is a classic example of the pursuit of a better future for your children and grandchildren. One of my favorite stories is my mother telling of the time when the presence of God showed up in a little rural Methodist church in Scottsbluff, Nebraska. People lay on the floor and bowed at the altar as healing broke out. She said, "God's presence was so thick you could cut it with a knife." Not metaphorically either. The tangible presence of God has always stirred my heart. That story and others like it may be the very seeds that have come to sprout in the ideas presented in this book. Thanks Mom and Dad! I love you.

ISBN-13: 978-1482011265 ISBN-10: 1482011263 Printed in the United States of America

CONTENTS

PART I
KILLING THE
SACRED COWS

INTRODUCTION

Raising Alexander

As I write, in January 2013, the United States of America is 16 trillion dollars in debt. When I ponder those numbers, I can't help but wonder if it is an amount that our economy can ever recover from. Honestly, I have no concept of 16 trillion dollars. Add to this the fact that millions of homes have been foreclosed on in the past two years due to the loose lending habits of our nation's banks. The easy lending practices caused a false real estate boom that resulted in a bubble effect in the inflated values of the homes. The bubble popped, the houses devalued, and many people found themselves stuck with mortgages that were double the market value of their homes. So they gave the homes back to the bank—millions of homes.

What do these problems have in common? The answer is simple: a shortsighted mindset with no regard for our children's future. The bigger question is *how did we get here as a society?* What ideas and beliefs have been fed into our culture that caused an entire generation of middle aged adults to take no regard for their grandchildren's future? It is a historical fact that a weak economy even threatens the safety and security of a nation.

I believe that the Church in America is partly to blame for this situation. It is we who are supposed to be the salt of the Earth. If we lose are saltiness, we are as Jesus said: "good for nothing" (see Matt. 5:13). How did we lose our saltiness? What is it that we failed to preserve? The answer is simple——hope! We failed to preserve hope for a better future.

I was brought up in a Christian home and eventually committed my heart to Jesus in 1980 at a Bob Dylan concert. If I combine the thirty-two years of my adult Christianity with the twelve years of my childhood growing up in a Nazarene Church, I can honestly say I experienced two constant themes in American Christianity: 1) Jesus saves, and 2) We are in the last days.

I love to read, and until two years ago, I was a media junkie. From the wide variety of books I've consumed, I can attest to the undisputed fact that the past fifty years of Christianity in America have been dominated by an end-times apocalyptic message. Every time a war breaks out, the Church proclaims, "This might be the end!" Every time a recession hits, we fear the economy of the antichrist is about to take over. Every time a European country has an economic slump or a protest in the streets, we teach the antichrist is about to be revealed. It has been non-stop my entire life. I grew up with the ever-present thought in the back of my mind that my children or my grandchildren will no doubt be the last generation on Earth.

In the meantime, the environmental movement has been shouting "Save the Earth," the technology world has been bridging the global communication gap, and the medical world has been increasing the lifespan of the average human being. The irony is that we the Church are the ones who are supposed to preserve the world with our salt-like impact. Instead, we have built into the subconscious mind of those who hear our message the belief that time is short, Jesus is coming, and the world as we know it is about to end. This dynamic was aggravated to new heights during the year 2012 because the much-publicized ancient Mayan calendar stops on the date December 21, 2012. The entire year seemed to have apocalypse in the air.

As a result of our last days fervor, an entire nation has mortgaged away the future of its grandchildren's children and compromised the security of what was once the mightiest country on the planet. Our prophets of doom have sold millions of books, our pastors have endorsed their message, and our children have lost hope.

I say *enough is enough!* We have no idea when Jesus is coming back! In fact, as you will discover in this book, a host of Bible prophecies have yet to be fulfilled before the Lord returns. The completion of these events could take hundreds of years. Yet American churchianity has somehow equated the rise and fall of our own nation's economy and morality with a sign that the world is ending. The preachers across this land have somehow come to believe that we are a prophetic indicator of the last days events. *We are not!* We are simply a nation that was founded on Judeo-Christian values and that has been extremely blessed by God. And I believe that if we stop preaching things we cannot prove (and could not possibly know) and start training our children to believe in a better future and a revived America, we have a great chance of coming out of the mess we are in.

If I have learned one thing in my years as a Christian, a pastor, and a Bible teacher, it is this—we can be very convincing about almost any kind of theology or eschatology we want. Any good preacher with enough time and preparation can make the Bible say just about anything he wants. At this point I will confess; I want to see hope restored in my children's future, and I am going to use the Bible to prove my case. I have come to understand the power of a prophetic voice and the authority it carries, and I will use mine for the sake of my children, steering the ship of Christianity toward a

13

better world. As the Bible tells us, *"Behold, children are a heritage from the Lord, the fruit of the womb is a reward. Like arrows in the hand of a warrior, so are the children of one's youth"* (Ps. 127:3–4). The question is: In what direction do we want to shoot our arrows? When we tell our children the world is ending, we are shooting our arrows into the ground.

One of history's most ambitious figures was no doubt Alexander the Great. Considering that many scholars believe he was the powerful, conquering Ram of Daniel 8:1–8, we can even say that his conquest shaped Old Testament prophecy. Look at what several historians say about the impact of Alexander's parents upon his ability to be a world- changer:

> Some of Alexander's strongest personality traits formed in response to his parents. His mother had huge ambitions, and encouraged him to believe it was his destiny to conquer the Persian Empire. Olympias' influence instilled a sense of destiny in him.1

> Plutarch tells us that his ambition "kept his spirit serious and lofty in advance of his years." However, his father Philip was Alexander's most immediate and influential role model, as the young Alexander watched him campaign practically every year, winning victory after victory while ignoring severe wounds.2

Mothers, fathers, grandparents, preachers, teachers, authors, screenwriters—let's get back to hope. If we do, we will change the next generation, and we will impact the future for good! This book is an attempt to begin that process by reshaping our end-times message and eschatology. I have sought at every turn to interpret future things through the lens of God's goodness, Jesus's love for the world, and the Church's potential to bring about change, favor, and blessing. At the same time, I have not abandoned the obvious realities that one day Jesus will return and that Satan will be exterminated from this Earth. It is part of God's plan. I only want to expand our thinking in terms of how influential we can be in that process, and I want to re-examine our position in the timeline in hopes that we can admit we have been too hasty in our prophetic end-time declarations. Thank you for buying this book; I don't think you'll regret it.

1. The Shaping of My Eschatology

During my childhood, my father embraced Aryan-racist so-called Christian ideals. His mixing of *Soldier of Fortune* magazines with Bible reading created a rather unattractive attitude about the world in relation to Christianity. He stockpiled guns and ammo—just in case the government turned against us or the antichrist arose to global supremacy and we had to head for the hills to wait out the Great Tribulation. Thankfully, my father eventually saw the error of his fearful and separatist worldview. He passed away May 18, 2007, totally in love with both Jesus and the world around him. I am not making a case against collecting guns or storing food but rather exposing how bad ideas mixed with Scripture can undermine the message of love and hope that Jesus brought to the world, replacing them with fear and hatred. My dad was known for being a very sensitive and generous man, but fear-based eschatology robbed him of those attributes for many years of his life.

Because of this part of my upbringing, I became acutely sensitive to Christian end-time scare tactics and sensationalism. Fast forward a few years to my early to mid-twenties. For six years, my wife, Doreen, and I attended the Calvary Chapel Costa Mesa church, and our children attended the associated Maranatha Christian Academy. One of the major underpinnings of the entire framework of the Calvary Chapel movement—the movement I would eventually become a pastor in—was an emphasis on end-times theology. For example, in 1986, a rock band connected to the movement, the Daniel Amos band, recorded an album called *The Revelation,* which included narration and reading from the book of Revelation. I attended a live concert of the entire album, with narration between songs. It was obviously intended as a teaching tool for end-time theology. While I'm not knocking the concept, it does illustrate well the high priority the Jesus People movement under the informal leadership of Calvary Chapel Costa Mesa placed on the end- times as a central theme of the message of the gospel.

In contrast to my post-apocalypse young adult upbringing, Calvary Chapel taught with emphasis the idea that the entire Church—all Christians everywhere—will be caught up in the air to meet Jesus prior to the events written about in the book of Revelation. I was attracted to the idea and the attitude that came from this view at the time. There was no fear of having to run for the hills and fight off the armies of the Beast. Instead, there was a huge emphasis on looking for what they called the *imminent* return of Jesus in the form of the Rapture, a snatching-away experience. Focusing on the coming of Christ was bright and cheery. It felt good. After all, what Christian doesn't want Jesus to come?

THE IMMINENT MINDSET

One of the hallmark texts for the imminent view of Jesus's return is Second Peter 3:10–14. (My added emphasis shows the words and phrases that apply.)

> ***But the day of the Lord will come as a thief in the night,*** *in which the heavens will pass away with a great noise, and the*

*elements will melt with fervent heat; both the earth and the works that are in it will be burned up. Therefore, since all these things will be dissolved, what manner of persons ought you to be in holy conduct and godliness, **looking for and hastening the coming of the day of God,** because of which the heavens will be dissolved, being on fire, and the elements will melt with fervent heat? Nevertheless we, according to His promise, look for new heavens and a new earth in which righteousness dwells. Therefore, beloved, looking forward to these things, be diligent to be found by Him in peace, without spot and blameless* (2 Peter 3:10–14).

In this passage is the principal belief that is the key to understanding the mainstream mindset of the pre-tribulation Rapture, also known as the *futurist* position. The belief is that Jesus Christ could come at any moment, *but* the return that is imminent is the Rapture (the catching away of the Church before the Great Tribulation), *not* the triumphant Final Return of Jesus Christ.

Along with this view came the idea that, prior to the Rapture of the Church, the very institution of Christianity would become tainted by false prophets and deceptive miracles. This caused much (if not most) of western Christendom to become skeptical toward any manifestations of the Holy Spirit, including healing miracles, prophecy, and encounters with the presence of God that produced unusual behavior. For years, my family embraced this belief as part of our end-times package.

DITCHING DEFEATISM

Then in 2001, my seventh year as a full-time pastor, I began to feel dissatisfied with the very view I had been teaching. Although, to this day I still hold to the pre-tribulation Rapture view I agreed with the opponents of the Rapture who have rightly pointed out that it has bred a defeatist mindset within the Church. That was exactly what I found myself bumping my head up against. I am a rogue at heart. And I just couldn't swallow, any longer, the idea that the Church of the end-times will be small, weak, and of "little strength." As I began to wrestle with the idea of the imminent return of Jesus, I struggled to imagine the Lord of the harvest claiming a teeny and feeble Church as His prize. The very God-given instincts within me told me that the Jesus I know is going to produce a glorious and victorious work on this Earth despite all Satan's attempts at destruction. The whole point of the Church and Christianity is that a company of people would be spiritually born into a Kingdom, make disciples of nations, and respond with power against Satan's agenda. This idea began to foster an attitude within me that caused me to start questioning much of what I had been trained to think.

In 2009, as I was studying to teach through the book of Revelation for the third time, I realized that every time I researched the eschatology I had been trained in, I had more questions than answers. By contrast, when I would ditch the dispensationalist talking points and just read the book, I found more hope and simpler explanations. During that time I also noticed that skepticism toward the manifestations that often accompany miracles had paved the way for an eschatology that believed that, prior to the return of Jesus Christ, the Church will fall into deception and become susceptible to false signs and wonders instigated by Satan. Considering this belief, it was no surprise that much of the Church had shied away from anything that smelled like supernatural phenomena. The more I considered this, the more dissatisfied I felt. *No*, I reasoned, *this cannot be the Church that Jesus died for. This cannot be the end result of His plan. There is no way He is coming for the Church in our current condition.*

REGAINING POSSESSION OF THE BALL

I came to realize that not only had this defeatist mindset produced skepticism toward the use of spiritual gifts, but it had placed the Church on defense and Satan on offense. It was as though we were in the final seconds of a basketball game, we were down by one point, and Satan had the ball. Our goal was to stop the devil from scoring. But in a frustratingly ironic twist, while playing hard defense, we knew we were losing and, therefore, we expected the Rapture at any moment. Our only hope in this proverbial game was not to score the winning point but to disappear before the final buzzer. This doesn't fit with Jesus's words to Peter in Matthew 16:18, *"On this rock I will build My church, and the gates of Hades shall not prevail against it."*

As this verse clearly shows, we are supposed to be on the offensive, bashing in the gates of hell! It is we, the church who have possession of the ball, not Satan!

This basketball scenario isn't just a nice analogy. It was my personal reality as one who lived many years in the constant tension of an end-time theology that believes Satan will be more powerful than the Church. I was a Senior and Senior Associate pastor for sixteen years under the cloud of this eschatology, and it was a frustrating time for me personally. While I thoroughly enjoyed teaching the Bible, I felt like a recruiter for a losing team on the ground—one that had only a distant hope for victory at the end. I found comfort and justification in Bible verses such as Romans 8:36, which says, *"As it is written: 'For Your sake we are killed all day long; we are accounted as sheep for the slaughter.'"* This verse resonated with me due to my belief that the Church would be like a fighter on the ropes, our heads buried in our arms as we took our hits from the world, the flesh, and the devil. When I read Paul's description of the full armor of God in Ephesians 6, I would zero in on the phrase *"and having done all, to stand"*—— imagining myself reeling back and forth on my feet, doing all I could to stay on my feet while I waited for the Rapture bell to ring and rescue me from this losing battle.

To enforce this anemic end-time Church theology, we would commonly teach that the church of Philadelphia, described in Revelation 3, was a type of the last days Church on Earth just prior to the Rapture:

> *See,* ***I have set before you an open door,*** *and no one can shut it;* ***for you have a little strength, have kept My word, and have not denied My name.*** *Indeed I will make those of the synagogue of Satan, who say they are Jews and are not, but lie—indeed I will make them come and worship before your feet, and to know that I have loved you.* ***Because you have kept My command to persevere, I also will keep you from the hour of trial which shall come upon the whole world, to test those who dwell on the earth.*** *Behold, I am coming quickly! Hold fast what you have, that no one may take your crown"* (Revelation 3:8–11).

According to this view, the *"open door"* was the Rapture. The phrases *"little strength"* and *"have kept my word"* referred to the weakened condition of those few faithful "Bible-teaching" churches. And Jesus's promise, *"I will keep you from the hour of trial which shall come upon the whole earth"* meant He would take the weakened but persevering Bible-teaching remnant out of this world before the Great Tribulation.

These years later, I see that this theology has become self-fulfilling in a way. Because many believe in a weak and impotent end-times Church, they have no real power in their lives either. They know how to study and teach the gifts of the Holy Spirit from a theological perspective, but they are so fearful of the abuse of these gifts and the atmosphere they might produce that gifts like tongues, prophecy, and healing are shoved into a tiny box labeled CAUTION! This attitude causes those under their leadership to follow their lead; instead of exercising their spiritual gifts, they exercise their option to suppress them.

ESCAPING THE SLAUGHTERHOUSE

For years I had believed the world and the Church were heading—down! After all, we are *"lambs led to slaughter"* who, after *"having done all to stand"* will *"have a little strength"* in the end because we *"kept"* the Word.

In Bill Johnson's book *When Heaven Invades Earth,* he perfectly sums up what I was experiencing:

> One of the tragedies of weakened identity is how it affects our approach to Scripture. Many if not most theologians make the mistake of taking all the good stuff contained in the Prophets and sweeping it under the mysterious rug called the Millennium. It's not my desire to debate that subject right now. But I do want to deal with our propensity to put off those things that require courage, faith and action to another period of time. The mistaken idea is this, if it is good it can't be for now. A cornerstone in this theology is that the condition of the church will always be getting worse and worse. Therefore tragedy in the church is just another sign of these being the last days. In a perverted sense the weakness of the church confirms to many that they are on the right course. The worsening condition of the world and the church becomes a sign to them that all is well.

I had a problem: My overarching perception of reality was crushing me inside. I felt like the captain of the Titanic. All the while, my heart burned with a desperate desire to experience the presence of God and to see Him perform the miracles the Bible talks about. I knew something was wrong. I wondered:

- How can my personal desire for more of God be bad?

- Why shouldn't a last days Church be massive and glorious?

- Why can't the Church become a witness to the lost and dying world of the goodness and the power of a loving God?

- Why shouldn't we walk in triumphant victory?

- If the God of the Bible is the God of the last days' harvest, why wouldn't a victorious God harvest a massive yield?

- If the devil is going to rise up in power, signs, and lying wonders, why wouldn't Christians who are filled with the Holy Spirit also rise up in greater power? Doesn't the Bible also say, *"...He who is in you is greater than he who is in the world"* (1 John 4:4)?

All my questions and inner conflict brought me to this conclusion: I was at war. My sinking ship eschatology presented a direct affront to my victorious Christ theology, my understanding of the good nature of God, and my desire to experience God's power. I could tolerate the conflict and its casualties no longer. Something in me needed to die, and something else needed to come to life.

Standing In The Gap

Today I find myself standing in an eschatological gap. And I believe many others are standing with me. I must live in hope. On one side, I admit that someday this current world must expire so we can get on with eternity and physical, face-to-face fellowship with Jesus Christ. But on the other side, I am aware that if I am not fully convinced the gospel has the power to solve the issues of this life *now* and create a better life for future generations, I stand a chance of failing my children and their children. I stand a chance of destroying their future because I failed to believe fully in the promises of God. Here's the reality: If we don't get happy and get hope, we could go down in history as a nut-job generation that believed the world was going to end when, in fact, we were on the brink of a glorious era for all of humanity. An era of peace and righteousness. An era of prosperity and advancement. I am so glad the Pilgrims, as they made their way to America, did not think the world was about to end. In actuality, they were escaping bad theology that was crushing their hope and dreams. Like them, we must move forward with tenacious hope.

Yes, many terrible realities exist in the world today, but much more good is happening. Yes, I believe that one day the Church will be caught up to meet the Lord in the air prior to the Great Tribulation. I believe that one day in the future Jesus Christ will return triumphantly, and I believe in a future brief period when this planet will experience great calamity as Satan and the demonic realm are routed from Earth. However, we have no idea when that is going to happen. Unfortunately, many of the current fathers of western Christianity have become proud of their intellectual ability, and they enjoy the attention their ministries get when they focus on the end-times. They just can't help themselves. Calamity, controversy, fear, and chaos sell!

On the flip side, there are others who do not take the book of Revelation literally or who apply it solely to past events, ignoring the global and universal magnitude and scope of its prophecies. None of these stances has, in my opinion, satisfactorily explained the end-times prophecies of the Bible. Unfortunately (or fortunately, depending on our views), our Christian worldview is driven by our end-times views. Whether explicit or implicit, our eschatology has a major influence on how we do church, how we do missions, how we do evangelism, and how we worship God. For years, I had a positive Jesus but a negative future. Many still live in that place but are restless and hungry for something *different*, and I believe that different starts with adding hope to our view of the end-times and power to our view of the Church.

THE EMPEROR HAS NO CLOTHES

This book is nothing more than one man's idea—a departure from current schools of end-time thought with an eye on what I see happening right in front of my face. When it comes to the past fifty years of end- time theology, the emperor has no clothes! I want to offer another, more plausible and what I consider realistic view of the end-times.

The contents of this book are not a closed case. I am not arrogant enough to say I am absolutely right. No one person or movement has a completely accurate interpretation of the future prophecies of the Bible. No single movement within the Church has perfect eschatology or theology, either. This is my personal position at this time, but I am open to other views, and I refuse to be dogmatic.

Because I am unaware of any similar interpretations, I am relying solely on my own revelatory instincts. I am not offering a closed case, but a hypothesis. Thus, my commentary on the book of Revelation (Part II of this book) is not an exhaustive one. Rather, I offer a hybrid of traditional views, ignoring (for the most part) the usual arguments and instead following my heart and my hope.

I am simply attempting to sort out the plethora of possibilities regarding things to come. I believe any biblical position or interpretation that can be shaken *should* be shaken, and I believe my views are as biblically sound and plausible as the next person's. Yet I approach this subject with an awareness of my own humanity. Nothing frightens me more than Christians who have all the answers. I do not want to be one of those. For this reason, I place a high value on the mystery of *what-if* and the principal that God's Word runs much deeper than our human ability to anticipate it and perfectly interpret it.

In Alexander Venter's book *Doing Healing,* he writes:

Harvard theologian Krister Stendahl said: "It is not so much what we do not know, but what we think we know, that obstructs our vision" and eventually cripples us. If we are honest and teachable about what we do not know, tentative and explorative about what we think we know, and humble and responsible with what we do know, the world would be a different place. What Jesus did and taught provoked the prejudice, presumption and pride of the Pharisees and Jewish leaders. They opposed Him at every turn on the basis of what they thought they knew about what God could or could not do. This blinded them to "the time of Gods visitation", causing them to reject and oppose the salvation of God offered in Messiah. They thought they knew it all, but their "knowledge" destroyed them.2

This statement quoted in Alexander's book is a keen observation of the unfortunate, ongoing saga of Christian theological pride. God gave us end-times prophecy in His Word; therefore, we can assume He wants us to work through it, but never at the risk of blindness to actual outcome and fulfillment nor the compromise of His commands for the mission at hand. We must learn to embrace mystery, walk lightly and humbly, and rely on the goodness of God to light the way.

In light of this, I have coined two phrases that describe two of the Church's modern and historical Achilles' heels. We have a history of getting hung up on *prophetic dogmatism* and *end-times over-reactionism,* which I define in this way:

Prophetic dogmatism—A pre-textual approach to eschatology that results in a rigid and dogmatic approach to interpreting Bible prophecy and causes people to be unwilling to veer outside of one particular school or camp of eschatology.

End-times over-reactionism—A tendency to react prematurely to cataclysmic events, storms, and political and economic shifts, interpreting them as signs of the last days. This is not to say these events are never a sign of the times. However, many over-react in an effort to prove their eschatology instead of waiting for things to play out.

KINGDOM SHIFT

As I write, the Earth is in the midst of a huge shift socially, technologically, economically, and politically. As a result, much of the western Church is waiting for a revived Roman empire to produce an antichrist and implement the mark of the Beast. I don't think it's going to happen that way! I also am convinced that Jesus will not return today or tomorrow! Instead, I believe we are in the beginning stages of the largest influx of new believers into the Kingdom of Jesus Christ— ever! And the epicenter of this could be a place least expected.

As I mentioned before, the reason eschatology is so important is because it determines the lens through which we view the rest of life, including our Christian mission here on Earth. Let me propose a superior lens. We are under direct orders from Jesus to undo the works of Satan, and anything that distracts or deviates from that mission is not good theology or eschatology. Here's what Jesus said to His disciples:

> *And as you go, preach, saying, "The kingdom of heaven is at hand." Heal the sick, cleanse the lepers, raise the dead, cast out demons. Freely you have received, freely give* (Matthew 10:7–8).

> *And Jesus came and spoke to them, saying, "All authority has been given to Me in heaven and on earth. Go therefore and make disciples of all the nations, baptizing them in the name of the Father and of the Son and of the Holy Spirit,* **teaching them to observe all things that I have commanded you;** *and lo, I am with you always, even to the end of the age." Amen* (Matthew 28:18–20).

Here we see our commission and our goal—a great harvest of the lost. I begin this book with the assumption that, prior to the Church finally overcoming the sting of death at the event we call the Rapture, we will experience a massive, global influx into the Kingdom of Heaven. This must be our lens.

Whether you believe in a pre-Tribulation Rapture, a post-Tribulation Rapture, a no-Tribulation Rapture, a no-Rapture Tribulation, or some other scenario—if you are not hoping for a greater expression of God's Kingdom here on Earth and the possibility of a better future for all humanity, then you are a Church defeatist. You have decided that no future generation could possibly bring the gospel to the world better than your generation, that you have discovered all there is to discover about God's Word, and that, in regards to prophecy, no stones are left unturned. If this is you, on your best day, the greatest inheritance you have to offer your grandchildren is instruction on how to sink the ship!

Yet when you pass away, your children and grandchildren will rise up in your place and do for themselves the things your worldview kept you from even considering. They will throw out the ship-sinking instructions, and by their own desire for survival and the guidance of the Holy Spirit, they will create a better world. They will stamp out world hunger. They will stop terrorism; they will defeat communism; and they will bring the authentic gospel that demonstrates God's love and power to the entire world. I believe they will do this, with God's help, because it is His destiny for this world and because they will ask God for things you were afraid to ask for.

"I WOULD BLESS ME..."

Two years ago, during a time of prayer, something radically shifted in me. I was so tired of approaching God as a lowly sinner saved by grace. I had said, "I am nothing," and, "God You are everything," so many times that I realized God had turned His face away from me. I was a self-flagellating intercessor, and God was not impressed. It dawned on me that if the Lord is going to accomplish His will on Earth, according to the way He has already set in motion, *He needs me.*

I stood up and looked into Heaven and said, "If I were You, God, I would bless me!"

I was shocked at what had just come out of my mouth. But I began to repeat it, and I felt life on the words. I knew I had God's attention.

Then I said, "You know, Lord, that I want to serve You and please You and tell the world about You."

I went on and on explaining to the Lord why I believed it was in His interest to bless me, my life, and my family. And He did! He blessed me beyond my imagination!

What happened to me in this encounter is what I believe the Church of tomorrow is going to experience. Please hear my heart. I'm not insinuating God has deep unmet emotional needs that only I can fill, or that he cant carry out His plan without me, but! He has determined that humanity take part in His plan of redeeming the world. He wants us to co-labor with Him. Therefore it is essential we realize who we are and what we carry. We must come to a fuller understanding of God's desire and our essential role in His plan. And if we—the Christians and ministry leaders of this generation—do not get on board, Church history will not be kind to us.

When we who are God's children come fully into the realization of who we are and what they carry, then I believe the Lord will induce conditions on the planet to cause revival. And He won't use calamity or indiscriminant destruction to do so. It saddens me to hear what many of the prophets in America speculate about a particular storm or hurricane. They label tragedy as God's calling card, thus undermining the work and the power of the cross. When James and John wanted to command fire to come down from Heaven on the unreceptive Samaritans, Jesus rebuked them, saying, *"You do not know what manner of spirit you are of"* (Luke 9:55).

With this in mind, I have held to these tenants as the foundation of my eschatology of hope:

1. A better future and glorious hope for the world and the Church

2. A massive end-time harvest of souls

3. A unique interpretation of the book of Revelation

4. A powerful generation of supernatural believers who will be caught up into Heaven someday, thus never tasting the sting of death.

5. A failed attempt of Satan to establish dominion of the Earth.

6. A triumphant return of Jesus Christ

7. A thousand-year Jesus Kingdom on this Earth.

8. A distinct, honoring plan for the nation of Israel and the Jews

9. A new Heaven and Earth for all of eternity.

2. Would Jesus Return Tomorrow?

In the last chapter, I mentioned the importance of the doctrine of imminent return to much of modern end-time belief. Unfortunately, this belief has clouded the lens of end-time theology. Let's examine this idea more closely against the backdrop of Scripture and see if there is another view that can relieve all this end-time pressure that is driving much of Christianity into the ditch of fear-based evangelism.

In my personal experience and observation, the doctrine of the imminent return of Jesus Christ is a dominant belief in modern Christianity, and many denominations lean on it as a core value. I am not saying this is true of all or even most, but this belief is a core value of enough groups to have a major influence on the overall expression and attitude of the global body of Christ. Without dishonor for the millions of people who live out their daily lives with a view toward our coming King, and out of respect for the ministries around the world who work with a long-term view toward turning the world upside down for the gospel of Jesus Christ—I challenge this view.

First, we must distinguish between the fact that Jesus *could* come back today verses (if I may be so presumptuous) the reality that most of us do not honestly think He will. He *can* come back today because He is God, and God can do anything. But He won't come back today because the very job the Church has been commissioned to do is far from over.

In our modern age, many have believed that our technological advances have enabled us to be very close to fulfilling Jesus's words in Matthew 24:14: *"And this gospel of the kingdom will be preached in all the world as a witness to all the nations, and then the end will come."* However, the fact that we can broadcast the contents of the gospel message in nearly every language in the world or drop tracts from balloons across international borders does not mean we have *actually* spread the gospel. I am not saying we shouldn't do those things, but simply pointing out that those kinds of efforts are not in and of themselves complete representations of the gospel. The fact that a young boy can stuff his toys under the bed doesn't mean he has cleaned his room. Putting the Bible in someone's hands is not synonymous with spreading the gospel.

According to the New Testament, the gospel is spread by preaching, teaching, healing, casting out demons, and various other miraculous proofs of God's power and presence. Unfortunately, the Church has historically had an aversion toward such manifestations of God. Based on this alone, I honestly believe we are not even close to the coming of Jesus Christ, but if we can get over our hang-ups and offenses about the things we don't understand about the manifest presence of God, there is a chance that our children's children just might be the generation to usher in the coming of the Lord. Here's the reality: We are not waiting on Jesus; He is waiting on us. Our toys are under the bed, and our dirty laundry is stuffed in the closet, yet all the while, we are claiming our room is clean.

READINESS VS. IMMINENT RETURN

Although I am convinced the Lords return isn't any time soon, I do understand the value of our own individual need for readiness. Jesus stressed the importance of watching for Him.

And you yourselves be like men who wait for their master, when he will return from the wedding, that when he comes and knocks they may open to him immediately. Blessed are those servants whom the master, when he comes, will find watching. Assuredly, I say to you that he will gird himself and have them sit down to eat, and will come and serve them. And if he should come in the second watch, or come in the third watch, and find them so, blessed are those servants. But know this, that if the master of the house had known what hour the thief would come, he would have watched and not allowed his house to be broken into. Therefore you also be ready, for the Son of Man is coming at an hour you do not expect (Luke 12:36–40).

These verses clearly highlight the importance of a lifestyle of readiness. However, this does not mean that His return is, in fact, imminent. We should all live in constant readiness to meet the Lord at His coming, yet as two thousand years of history has shown, His coming may not be in our lifetimes.

Even the apostle Paul seems to stave off this notion among the Thessalonians. He wrote to them a not-yet exhortation addressing their concerns about Christ's return, and he gave some indicators as to the general events and global conditions of the time when the Lord will return. He spoke specifically of both the Rapture ("our *gathering together to Him"*) and the final return of Christ; they are synonymous yet separate events.

*Now, brethren, **concerning the coming of our Lord Jesus Christ and our gathering together to Him,** we ask you, not to be soon shaken in mind or troubled, either by spirit or by word or by letter, as if from us, as though the day of Christ had come. Let no one deceive you by any means; for that Day will not come **unless the falling away comes first,** and the man of sin is revealed, the son of perdition, who opposes and exalts himself above all that is called God or that is worshiped, so that he sits **as God in the temple of God,** showing himself that he is God. Do you not remember that when I was still with you I told you these things? And now you know what is restraining, that he may be revealed in his own time. For the mystery of lawlessness is already at work; only He who now restrains will do so until He is taken out of the way. And then the lawless one will be revealed, whom the Lord will consume with the breath of His mouth and destroy with the brightness of His coming. The coming of the lawless one is according to the working of Satan, with all power, signs, and lying wonders, and with all unrighteous deception among those who perish, because they did not receive the love of the truth, that they might be saved. And for this reason God will send them strong delusion, that they should believe the lie, that they all may be condemned who did not believe the truth but had pleasure in unrighteousness* (2 Thessalonians 2:1–12).

Here Paul made it very clear that Christ's gathering of the Church has some preconditions. He then talked about a future "falling away" (apostasia) and several other preconditions to the return of the Lord so as to steer the Thessalonians away from abandoning their post. He encouraged them, "You'll know when it's time, but it's not time yet, and this is how we know that." A few verses later, he encouraged them to *"stand fast and hold the traditions which you were taught, whether by word or by epistle"* (2 Thess. 2:15). Later, in the third chapter, Paul continued this line of thinking by saying:

*We have confidence in the Lord concerning you, both that you do and will do the things we command you. Now may the Lord direct your hearts into the love of God and into the **patience** of Christ* (2 Thessalonians 3:4–5).

This is crucial to my entire thesis on this matter. While Jesus emphasized a readiness state of mind, the apostles He appointed stressed a patience so as to remain focused on the commands of Jesus and the apostolic leadership. In other words, we must hold these two truths in tension. We must live our lives in a constant state of readiness to meet Jesus, even when we know His return is not yet. And we must also be patient and keep our focus on expanding the Kingdom on Earth and preparing the world for Christ's return.

We can live in this tension because the Bible has given us clear signs that will help us identify when these events are nearing. Paul spells some of these out in First Thessalonians 2, referencing a "falling away" and a "lawless one" who will seduce many into his lawless ways. Many believe and teach that Paul was referring to the antichrist. However, the antichrist is not a certain individual. Rather, the Bible speaks of the spirit of antichrist, who was already at work in Paul's day and continues its work today (see 1 John 2:18,22; 4:3; 2 John 1:7). Revelation speaks of a Beast, which is a confederation of nations, a False Prophet, which speaks on behalf of the Beast, and an image of the Beast, which is an idol representing the Beast. But nowhere in the book of Revelation do we find an antichrist person, per se.

Aside from whom the antichrist may or may not be, I believe Paul was kicking the can down the road in order to refocus the Thessalonian church on the present mission of spreading the Kingdom. Unfortunately, much confusion exists regarding exactly what kind of conditions Paul described in Second Thessalonians 2:1-12.

However, Paul describes the sequence by saying, *"The lawless one will be revealed, whom the Lord will consume with the breath of His mouth and destroy with the brightness of His coming"* (2 Thess. 2:8). This connects the *"lawless one"* and the *"apostasy"* to the future return of Jesus. If the lawless one was Caesar Nero or Titus, as some have concluded, how will they be *"destroyed with the brightness of His coming"* since they have already died? It appears to me that Paul kicked the proverbial can of Christ's return way down the road. And since Christ hasn't returned yet and the Rapture hasn't happened, I am on safe ground. It seems obvious to me that these scenarios *in their entirety* are yet to happen. For this reason, I conclude that Paul intentionally deferred the coming of the Lord to a much later era than the one they were currently living in. And I am doing the same.

COMING YET PRESENT

Paul wasn't the only one who did this. I believe this was the general position of the early apostles. The book of James provides another excellent example:

> *Therefore be patient, brethren, until the coming of the Lord. See how the farmer waits for the precious fruit of the earth, waiting patiently for it until it receives the early and latter rain. You also be patient. Establish your hearts, for the coming of the Lord is at hand* (James 5:7–8).

Here James emphasized patience by speaking in agricultural terms. He wanted his readers to understand, from a heavenly perspective, that the "farmer" waits until after the "latter rain." The phrase *latter rain* is commonly used in the charismatic movement today to describe the last days outpouring of the Holy Spirit. Yet the next sentence appears to introduce a conundrum. James said, *"Establish your hearts, for the coming of the Lord is at hand,"* as if to contradict himself all in the same breath.

I propose James was actually saying that the return of Jesus won't come until after the latter rain (end-time worldwide revival) but that the believers should *"establish"* (strengthen) their hearts because the *presence* of the Lord was near (at hand, within reach). The Greek phrase translated as *"coming of the Lord is at hand"* is *perousia kyrios eggizo*. This can also be translated in English as "the presence of whom you belong to is drawing near."1 In other words, Jesus's return is not in the near future, but His presence is within reach.

Ironically when Jesus said, *"Repent, for the kingdom of heaven is at hand,"* in Matthew 4:17, He spoke in similar terms, referring to the immediate access of the presence and power of God that was made available at His first coming. Both of these statements merge the future with the present. And combined, these two seemingly separate statements create what appears to me to be a unique correlation between the coming of the Lord and the presence of His Kingdom.

FRIENDLY FIRE

Much of the present end-time confusion about Jesus's return has caused many theologians and preachers to begin accusing other parts of the Church of being apostate and antichrist. Like an over-anxious lynch mob, they readily identify this group or that group as false prophets of the last days who are performing false signs. They believe that when Paul said that there will be a "falling away" he was referring to a portion of the Church moving away from sound teaching and biblical doctrines. In their zeal to expedite the return of

Jesus, they have postured their view against the Church itself and against the movement of the Spirit in the Earth.

Many "watch-dog" ministries in the Church today are saying that much of mainstream Christianity itself is headed into apostasy/falling away. And these sound doctrines are, of course, a replica of their own beliefs with little or no scrutiny applied to their own institutions and preferred denominations.

Sadly, these "watch-dogs" are ruining the atmosphere that is essential for a glorious and victorious future Church. Because so many of them are opposed to the supernatural side of Christianity—including healing, prophecy, and the like—they have labeled much of the charismatic movement as apostate. The reality is that these people do not know the difference between real signs and wonders and false signs and wonders because they have *zero experience* in the miraculous. To learn how to discern between false signs and wonders and real signs and wonders, one should probably hang around places where genuine signs and wonders are taking place.2

My own story verifies this. I was trained to be skeptical of claims of healing and other supernatural events. I even taught others to do the same for sixteen and a half years. Then I had a close-up view of these phenomena, only to discover that my peers had unintentionally misled me. I had allowed others to make up my mind for me without actually doing my own hands-on research. When I finally did my research, I discovered that the very things I had criticized—like people being slain in the spirit, people being filled with so much joy that they can't stop laughing, and people shaking under God's power—are legitimate God encounters that have a tremendous impact on the health, love, and compassion of people. Those who had these experiences produced undeniable fruit in their lives and their love for God and His Word.

The critics who are opposed to the supernatural lifestyle have decided that studying the Bible is all that is needed to be the Church. This reminds me of what Jesus said in Luke 11:52, *"Woe to you lawyers! For you have taken away the key of knowledge. You did not enter in yourselves, and those who were entering in you hindered."*

Ironically, the "falling away" Paul referred to in Second Thessalonians 2 could not have been in reference to the Church but to *"those who perish, because they did not receive the love of the truth that they might be saved"* (2 Thess. 2:10). As far as I know, all of Christianity has a love and devotion to the truth. It is that very thing that actually stirs up the division among us. Paul was speaking specifically in reference to those who are dying because of their disregard for God. It saddens me that we Christians can be so quick to condemn other believers when we see or hear of things we haven't experienced or don't understand. A sad result of this reality is a resistance to the very move of the Holy Spirit that is essential to bring global revival and subsequently the return of Christ.

We must get this through our heads: Believers in the Lord Jesus Christ *cannot* be the apostasy. This goes for the Catholic Church, too. They have been shamelessly branded as the apostate church, and the Pope has often been labeled the antichrist. Dave Hunt even goes so far as to label it the whore of Babylon in his book *The Woman Rides the Beast*. Ironically the same level and kinds of corruption that he has so meticulously documented in his indictment against Catholicism exist to varying degrees in the history of most Christian denominations. Jesus clearly pointed out in the seven letters to the churches in Revelation 1–3 that the Church can be lukewarm, misguided, carnal, materialistic and even seduced by Jezebel. But He still claims them as His Church. He even warns the church of Ephesus that, if they don't return to their first love, He will remove their lampstand. I believe this speaks of their light and effectiveness in the world. However, they are still His Church. (See 1 John 4:1-3)

In conclusion, since the Rapture and the final coming of Jesus are not imminent and the Church cannot be the apostates Paul described, I believe the Church will instead rise in power and influence in the world. We have much work to do before we're a powerful force for the Kingdom on the Earth. And Jesus, the ever-patient one, isn't coming back until we complete our mission. I believe that deep within the heart of every Christian abides a desire to see this world transformed and to see every human experience a fair and accurate representation of Jesus Christ. That is our Father's desire as well (see 2 Pet. 3:9). Like the farmer who awaits the latter rain, let us be patient and establish our hearts on the immediate reality that the presence of God is near.

VISITATIONS VS. COMINGS

Let me introduce another facet of Jesus coming that has been overlooked and, in most of traditional Christendom, totally disregarded. The fact is that Jesus has a history of personally visiting people and even groups of people that spans from His ascension until this very day. When Jesus spoke to the church of Laodicea in Revelation 3:14–22, He said *"Behold I stand at the door and knock. If anyone hears My voice and opens the door, **I will come in to him and dine with him,** and he with Me."* When He spoke to the church of Ephesus in Revelation 2:1–7, He said, *Nevertheless I have this against you, that you have left your first love. Remember therefore from where you have fallen; repent and do the first works, or else I will come to you quickly and remove your lampstand from its place—unless you repent.*

42

In both of these cases, Jesus spoke of personal visitations that would not be classified as His coming, but were nonetheless real encounters that could be expected based on the conditions and responses of both Laodicea and Ephesus.

The apostle Paul was likewise visited personally by Jesus on his famous Damascus Road conversion. Later, in First Corinthians 9:1 and 15:8, Paul admitted to having personal visitations. Similarly, when Paul spoke of his *"thorn in the flesh"* (2 Cor. 12:7), he records that Jesus spoke personally to him, saying *"My grace is sufficient for thee, for my strength is made perfect in weakness"* (2 Cor. 12:9). Here, I would like us to consider the possibility that, when Jesus spoke of the need for us to always be ready for Him, He was eluding to personal visitations as one of the ways we can expect Him. Not only are we to live in expectation of the Rapture and His triumphant final return, but we are also supposed to live in hope and expectation that Jesus could come to each one of us at any moment and have one-on-one fellowship with us. *It is His visitations that are imminent.* These could be private or corporate. Imagine what the entire family of Jesus Christ would be like if we each had personal Jesus encounters, one-on-one meetings with the King, who is also our best friend. I believe this is His desire for us.

On two separate occasions, both in 2010, I have had personal visitations from Jesus. The first was about forty-five minutes long. I could almost see His presence and discern His body language. The entire atmosphere of the room was transformed, and we talked like friends. The voice was not audible but I heard it (if that makes sense). Every time I started to cry, he would ask me to stop crying. He taught me from the book of Luke and told me how much he liked Peter and that He liked me, too. I am forever impacted by the fact that Jesus came to me to affirm our friendship and tell me personally that He liked me as a person. At the time, I had been in a season of desperation for His presence but had no idea how to get there. And to be honest, I really needed a friend. He also told me that from now on I would have to "learn to function in His presence." The second visitation happened a few months after that, when I was overtaken by the power of the Holy Spirit when a friend thrust his fist toward my stomach to impart the baptism of the Holy Spirit to me. After a few seconds of resisting the force that was pulling me down, I suddenly found myself lying on the floor as though I weighed a thousand pounds. I tried to get up but was unable to move. Jesus sat on me like an older brother, holding my hands down. He put His nose to my nose and said, "Stop resisting; it's Me, and I love you." He repeated it while what felt like low voltage electricity pulsed through my body. After that encounter, I began healing the sick and casting demons out of people as if it was second nature.

I share these to demonstrate that personal visitations from Jesus are intended to be part of our normal Christian experience. When it comes to visitations, I say, "Yes! Jesus could come at any moment, and I hope He does." However, the Rapture is another story. It is not happening any time soon, and neither is His triumphant return to claim this Earth. As I will show you later in this book, many awesome and wonderful things must happen first.

WHY? BECAUSE THERE IS MORE

The apostle Peter made reference to the need for patience, saying that people would mock the idea of the coming of the Lord because He seemed to be taking so long. Yet Peter defended the Lord's patience and long-suffering as an act of grace. In this passage, I believe he kicks the can even farther down the road than Paul did in his letter to the Thessalonians. While Paul seemed unsure about the timing of the Lord's return and alluded to it as a possibility only after a series of unfulfilled pre-conditions, Peter's letter (written fifteen years after Paul's) seems to defer the coming of the Lord to a much later time.

Knowing this first: that scoffers will come in the last days, walking according to their own lusts, and saying, "Where is the promise of His coming? For since the fathers fell asleep, all things continue as they were from the beginning of creation" (2 Peter 3:3–4).

The Lord is not slack concerning His promise, as some count slackness, but is long suffering toward us, not willing that any should perish but that all should come to repentance. But the day of the Lord will come as a thief in the night... (2 Peter 3:9–10).

Let's examine the *thief in the night* statement. This phrase has been used to add to the mystique and scare tactics of many preachers. In reality, it only means that Jesus's coming will be a surprise, and it will happen in stealth-like fashion. Considering the simplicity of this concept, we need to examine our use of this phrase. Could our zeal to see people make a decision for Christ cause us to manipulate Scripture a tad? I think so.

My overall point here is that, contrary to popular teaching, Peter wasn't using imminent return language. It is the opposite. Peter had a revelation that the Lord will even appear to be slack concerning His promise to come back, and history has proven this to be the case. Along the same lines, Jesus said in Matthew 24:32–33:

Now learn this parable from the fig tree: When its branch has already become tender and puts forth leaves, you know that summer is near. So you also, when you see all these things, know that it is near—at the doors!

45

Jesus taught here that we will be aware of the season. If this is the season of Christ's return—meaning He may return tomorrow—that means Jesus has accomplished all He can through His Church. I do not think any of us can honestly suggest the Church has completed her work on Earth to the satisfaction of Jesus Christ or that the harvest He died for is sufficient. Thus, looking at the signs, we can confidently say, *now is not the season*.

In Romans, Paul alludes to the consummation of God's redemptive plan as future and gives us a picture of what the Church will look like:

> *For all creation is waiting eagerly for that future day when God will reveal who his children really are. Against its will, all creation was subjected to God's curse. But with eager hope, the creation looks forward to the day when it will join God's children in glorious freedom from death and decay* (Romans 8:19–21 NLT).

Paul's statement here is one of the most ambiguous of all. He says that creation itself is waiting for a complete revelation of the identity of God's children. This tells me that something needs to happen that identifies us, marks us, or proves us. This single statement has huge prophetic implications. Is Heaven itself going to place a seal of endorsement on the Church that the world can see? I suggest that this, too, is yet to happen in its entirety.

Again, honesty requires us to admit *it's not time yet*. We need to change the way we talk, and we need to stop constantly telling the world that the end is near. We have no way of verifying that claim. As far as I am concerned, we are headed into a glorious time for the Church and the Earth. As people around the world are turned on to an authentic gospel of love and power, they will fall in love with King

Jesus, with Abba Father, and with Holy Spirit. As the Church, we are transitioning from a crawl to a walk. We are just beginning to realize the power of His presence and the presence of His power. And it is our awareness of the supernatural power of the Holy Spirit that is moving us forward into our glorious future. Our fullness is yet to come. Yes there is more. Encouraged?

3. Understanding the Abomination of Desolation, or Not

The Abomination of Desolation is an event written about by the prophet Daniel and repeated by Jesus to His disciples as He cautioned them about the coming destruction of the temple in Jerusalem. It is one of the more mysterious end-time events and has become the source of much speculation over the years. But what is it, really? Here is my very condensed explanation: When a conqueror of Jerusalem enters into a holy place and stops the daily rituals and sets up a detestable idol on an altar, that will be the Abomination of Desolation. Jesus said that when this happens, those living in the vicinity of this event should leave as quickly as possible.

> *As Jesus was leaving the Temple grounds, his disciples pointed out to him the various Temple buildings. But he responded, "Do you see all these buildings? I tell you the truth, they will be completely demolished. Not one stone will be left on top of another!" Later, Jesus sat on the Mount of Olives. His disciples came to him privately and said, "Tell us, when will all this happen? What sign will signal your return and the end of the world?" Jesus told them, "Don't let anyone mislead you"* (Matthew 24:2–4 NLT).

The remainder of Matthew 24 contains His response, including this mention of the Abomination of Desolation:

"Therefore when you see the 'abomination of desolation,' spoken of by Daniel the prophet, standing in the holy place" (whoever reads, let him understand), "then let those who are in Judea flee to the mountains. Let him who is on the housetop not go down to take anything out of his house. And let him who is in the field not go back to get his clothes. But woe to those who are pregnant and to those who are nursing babies in those days! And pray that your flight may not be in winter or on the Sabbath. For then there will be great tribulation, such as has not been since the beginning of the world until this time, no, nor ever shall be. And unless those days were shortened, no flesh would be saved; but for the elect's sake those days will be shortened. Then if anyone says to you, 'Look, here is the Christ!' or 'There!' do not believe it. For false christs and false prophets will rise and show great signs and wonders to deceive, if possible, even the elect. See, I have told you beforehand. Therefore if they say to you, 'Look, He is in the desert!' do not go out; or 'Look, He is in the inner rooms!' do not believe it. For as the lightning comes from the east and flashes to the west, so also will the coming of the Son of Man be. For wherever the carcass is, there the eagles will be gathered together (Matthew 24:15–28).

Jesus was referring to this prophecy from the Book of Daniel.

And he said, "Go your way, Daniel, for the words are closed up and sealed till the time of the end. Many shall be purified, made white, and refined, but the wicked shall do wickedly; and none of the wicked shall understand, but the wise shall understand. And from the time that the daily (sacrifice) is taken away, and the abomination of desolation is set up, there shall be one thousand two hundred and ninety days. Blessed is he who waits, and comes to the one thousand three hundred and thirty-five days" (Daniel 12:9–12; also see Daniel 9:26–27).

What Jesus is clearly saying is that when the Abomination of Desolation happens, those in Judea are to waste no time and get out of town because *"there will be great tribulation, such as has not been since the beginning of the world until this time, no, nor ever shall be"* (Matt. 24:21).

I'll admit it. This particular event, the Abomination of Desolation, is most puzzling to me. Jesus seemed to connect it to the very last days before His triumphant return. Notice that He describes tribulation unprecedented since the beginning of the Earth (kosmos). The use of the word *kosmos* links the events triggered by the Abomination of Desolation to global and even atmospheric proportions even though He seems to be speaking to *"those in Judea"* (Matt. 24:16). Here's my struggle with this prophecy: The various prophetic interpretations of the Abomination of Desolation are founded on so many assumptions that I find myself having to overlook a bunch of gaps and questions that arise to accept them. As far as I can tell, Scripture, history, and the various interpretations of this event raise way more questions than answers. This dynamic has led to a host of gap-filling interpretations by various theologians in an attempt to reconcile this event spoken of by Jesus. The two main positions are:

1. There has to be a Temple built in Jerusalem for the entire last days scenario of the book of Revelation to happen.

2. This entire event happened in AD 70, making it totally historical.

I will explain why I cannot accept any of the common explanations completely; thus my conclusions (or partial conclusions) by the end of this chapter will separate me from almost all of the other positions taken on this difficult prophecy. Regardless of your place in the spectrum, I hope you can enjoy the following debate that I seem to be having with myself. Perhaps it will spark some debate within you as well.

THE ALMOST FULFILLMENT

The discourse Jesus gave in Matthew 24:15-28 *seems* to have been fulfilled when Rome attacked Jerusalem and destroyed the temple in AD 70 under Titus—but this theory has a few big holes! As mentioned previously, the Abomination of Desolation is the setting up of an idol in the holy place or sanctuary, including actually desecrating the temple and putting a stop to daily rituals. Titus *kind of* fulfilled this prophecy when he destroyed the temple. And then there is another event, about 200 years before Jesus spoke these words, that happened under Antiochus Epiphanes and is *almost* a dead ringer for Daniel's prophecy. *Almost.*

TITUS

Concerning the events surrounding Titus's invasion of Jerusalem, here are some excerpts from the well-respected Jewish historian Josephus:

> But Titus said, that "although the Jews should get upon that holy house, and fight us thence, yet ought we not to revenge ourselves on things that are inanimate instead of the men themselves;" and that he was not in any case for burning down so vast a work as that was.

So he commanded that the chosen men that were taken out of the cohorts should make their way through the ruins and quench the fire.

And now Caesar was in no way able to restrain the enthusiastic fury of the soldiers, and the fire proceeded on more and more.

Yet were their passions too hard for the regard they had for Caesar, and the dread they had for him who forbade them, as was their hatred of the Jews.1

Here we see that the Roman soldiers destroyed the temple, yet Titus tried (unsuccessfully) to restrain the destruction of the temple (which was one of the great wonders of the ancient world). Certainly, this fact does not make or break the argument, but at the same time, Titus's image hardly fits the evil implicit in Daniel's prophecy.

Later, in Chapter VI, Josephus records:

And upon burning the holy house itself, and all of the buildings lying around about it, brought their ensigns to the temple, and set them over against the eastern gate; and there they did offer sacrifices to them, and there they did make Titus imperator with the greatest acclimations of joy.2

Here the soldiers sacrificed to their ensigns—the national flags and banners they carried into war with them. Yet these are not idols per se, and the worshippers were not *"standing in the holy place,"* like Jesus said, but at the east gate in the burned-out ruble. This, for me, is more of a case-breaker.

Also, in Matthew 24, Jesus seemed to be warning His audience as if they were going to witness this terrible event, but He also seemed to be tying it to His return. This obviously creates a significant inconsistency if we place the Abomination of Desolation in AD 70, so many years prior to Jesus's final return. Another frustrating and confusing element of this passage is found in Matthew's parenthetical aside to Jesus's words—"(whoever *reads, let him understand)."* What's up with that? Is He admitting the unique complexity of what he is prophesying? The details of Titus's destruction of the temple are *similar* to what the Bible tells us of the Abomination of Desolation, but they don't quite fit. For this reason, I find it hard to accept this event as the complete fulfillment of that prophecy.

To add weight to my argument against Titus being the one to carry out this deed (although he did participate, reluctantly, in the destruction of the temple) is the fact that Caesar Nero died approximately two years prior to the temple's destruction. This would eliminate Nero as the so-called antichrist since Daniel 9:26–27 tied the Abomination of Desolation to the coming "prince" who is commonly referred to as the antichrist. Therefore, Caesar Nero had nothing to do with and was obviously unable to attend what was supposed to be the antichrist's "coming out" party—the Abomination of Desolation.

ANTIOCHUS EPIPHANES

To add to the perplexity of this prophecy is the fact that Jesus quoted Daniel, who appeared to be prophesying about Antiochus Epiphanes, who carried out the prophecy of Daniel almost perfectly about 200 years before Jesus spoke the words of Matthew 24. Here's what Josephus wrote about Antiochus Epiphanes:

> [He] came upon the Jews with a great army, and took their city by force, and slew a great multitude of those that favored Ptolemy, and sent out his soldiers to plunder them without mercy. He also spoiled the temple, and put a stop to the constant practice of

offering a daily sacrifice of expiation for three years and six months.

Now Antiochus was not satisfied either with his unexpected taking of the city, or with its pillage, or with the great slaughter he had made there; but being overcome with his violent passions, and remembering what he had suffered during the great siege, he compelled the Jews to dissolve the laws of their country, and to keep their infants uncircumcised, and to sacrifice swine flesh upon the altar; against which they all opposed themselves, and the most approved among them were put to death.3

The prophecies of Daniel 7:25, 9:27, and 12:11 clearly seem to have been fulfilled by Antiochus Epiphanes. In fact, many futurist theologians go as far as saying that Antiochus is a *type of* antichrist and that this historical event is a foreshadowing of the future event.

I need you to see the complexity here. Jesus prophesied the soon coming destruction of Jerusalem's temple, connecting it to Daniel's prophecy about the Abomination of Desolation, which appears to have already been fulfilled by Antiochus Epiphanes. Then, to add to the dilemma, He connects it to His own Final Return. It's as if He stretched one single prophecy over the time span of two and a half thousand years and counting.

Evidence in Revelation

Another issue I have with the Abomination of Desolation is that I have a hard time finding it in the book of Revelation, where all the events of the end-times are foretold. Such an omission is difficult to understand. This is only magnified by the absence of other seemingly significant end-time details from Revelation—details like the antichrist (which I mentioned previously) and the rebuilt temple. If the book of Revelation is, as its title declares, a full disclosure and unveiling of the future, then why aren't these significant events mentioned?

Unfortunately, all of the muddled theories about the Abomination of Desolation—combined with an insistence that a single man will rise as the antichrist to carry out the Abomination of Desolation during the Great Tribulation—has fueled the theory that the temple in Jerusalem must be rebuilt before the time of the end. The antichrist will supposedly allow the rebuilding, entering into a covenant of some kind, but then he will break the covenant and fulfill the Abomination of Desolation, which will mark the middle of the Tribulation and cause the Jews to flee (fulfilling Jesus's warning in Matthew 24:15–28). *But* problems abound with this theory, too. In fact, I would go so far as to say that the insistence on a rebuilt temple in Jerusalem as a sign of the times is more of a distraction than a solid position.

If a temple will be rebuilt in Jerusalem during the Great Tribulation, I find it very strange that Revelation makes no mention of its construction and that it never describes an antichrist entering it (not to mention that it does not describe an antichrist at all). In Revelation 13:14, the people are told to *"make an image to the beast,"* and the next verse tells us this statue is given the power to speak. Yet no mention is made of where this image of the Beast speaks from. Revelation 16:10 speaks of the destruction of the Beast's throne, saying, *"Then the fifth angel poured out his bowl on the throne of the beast, and his kingdom became full of darkness...,"* yet still makes no mention of where this throne is. It seems to me that if the Beast's future throne will be in Jerusalem, it would have been an important detail for John to include. Instead, Revelation provides no location. It could be Jerusalem—or it could be Dubai, Brussels, or Nashville.

THE TEMPLE OBSESSION

Most scholars who examine the events surrounding the Abomination of Desolation have concluded that a temple must be built on Mount Zion for the Abomination of Desolation to happen. The logic is that this is the only way for the antichrist to enter the holy place. We know that a new temple will eventually exist, according to a prophecy from Ezekiel:

The Spirit lifted me up and brought me into the inner court; and behold, the glory of the LORD filled the temple. Then I heard Him speaking to me from the temple, while a man stood beside me. And He said to me, "Son of man, this is the place of My throne and the place of the soles of My feet, where I will dwell in the midst of the children of Israel forever..." (Ezekiel 43:5–7).

God promises to set the soles of His feet in this temple, where He will dwell eternally with the children of Israel. So it is clear that the building of a new temple is guaranteed, but the time frame is not. Maybe it will happen after Christ returns. My point is this: I am not totally convinced of the necessity of a rebuilt temple as a pivotal point in the end-times scenario. I am more concerned with the modern obsession with the idea.

Jesus spoke strongly and pointedly about a future temple that I believe will help us gain some perspective. Most of us are familiar with the incident when Jesus overturned the tables of the money changers in the temple. Notice what transpired immediately afterward in John 2:18–21:

*So the Jews answered and said to Him, "What sign do You show to us, since You do these things?" Jesus answered and said to them, "Destroy this temple, and **in three days I will raise it up."** Then the Jews said, "It has taken forty-six years to build this*

57

temple, and will You raise it up in three days?" But He was speaking of the temple of His body."

When Jesus prophesied this about the temple, John clarified that Jesus was speaking of the temple of His body. I agree with John, of course, but I believe Jesus was also speaking of the actual temple. Later, when Jesus was on trial prior to His crucifixion, one of the witnesses against Him said, *"This fellow said, 'I am able to destroy the temple of God and to **build it in three days'"** (Matt. 26:61). Again we read in Mark 14:58, *"We heard him say, 'I will destroy this temple that is made with hands, and **within three days I will build another made without hands.'"*** I am intrigued by Jesus's statement that another temple will be made without hands.

This connects to the time when the children of Israel were delivered from the attacking forces of Pharaoh's army at the famed Red Sea crossing; they responded with a beautiful song of deliverance, of which this is the last line:

*You will bring them in and plant them on Your own mountain— the place oh Lord reserved for Your own dwelling, the sanctuary, oh Lord, **that Your hands have established.** The Lord will reign forever and ever* (Exodus 15:17-18 NLT).

This leads me to consider the possibility that it may not be essential for a new temple to be rebuilt prior to the Great Tribulation or the return of Jesus Christ. Rather, I believe the new temple could be constructed without human hands—supernaturally—after Christ's return. It's just an idea.

THE OTHER "HOLY PLACE"

Let me propose another view that I am fully aware is a radical departure from all other potential scenarios. This starts with the premise of the Abomination of Desolation as a future event that triggers the very things that Daniel and Jesus talked about. As we've discussed, the prevailing belief is that a man, labeled as the antichrist, will be the one who commits the Abomination of Desolation. However, I have well- established in this book that the Bible does not speak of any single person as the antichrist. Rather, the antichrist is only mentioned in First and Second John, and these passages are broad references to anyone who is anti-Jesus or, more accurately, anti-anointed. As Second John 1:7 tells us, there are many antichrists.

From this we can see that, for the Abomination of Desolation to take place in the Tribulation, it would be the False Prophet, not an antichrist, who would enact the Abomination of Desolation by putting a stop to the daily routine of religious practices in the *"holy place."* The Beast can't do it because the Beast is a group of nations, not a person, and the image of the Beast can't do it because it is a statue. From the evil end-time line-up, only the False Prophet could possibly fit the role. Or it could be some other prominent political or religious figure.

Now let's consider the rituals being stopped during the Abomination of Desolation. If we read carefully the prophecies of Daniel about this event, we see that the daily ritual that is halted is not clearly defined (see Dan. 8:11–3; 11:31; 12:11). Many have read it to mean that the daily sacrifices will halt, but in this passage, the word *sacrifice* has been added by the translators. The original text does not say "daily *sacrifice"* but simply "daily." This addition of a single word has caused many theologians to believe this means a temple will be rebuilt on the Temple Mount in Jerusalem and the ancient Jewish practice of animal sacrifice will be re-instituted. This speculation has placed enormous emphasis on the need for a Jewish temple to be rebuilt in Israel—not a synagogue but a temple where sacrifices are done on the Temple Mount.

At this point, I want to do what I do so well—throw another stick in the spokes of this interpretation. Currently standing on the Temple Mount in Jerusalem is a Muslim holy place called, in English, the Dome of the Rock. This shrine is supposedly built atop the very rock where Muslims believe Abraham offered to slay his own son Isaac (see Gen. 22).4

Although the Dome of the Rock is not the Jewish temple, for all intents and purposes, it is a holy place. Thus, I wonder whether the Abomination of Desolation—shiqquwts *shamem* in Hebrew, which means "a detestable thing or idol that is appalling and horrific"5— could be fulfilled in this other "holy place." Certainly, if someone entered the Dome of the Rock and put a stop to the daily prayers of the Muslim world, placing a detestable and offensive idol on the rock and attempting to persuade the world to worship it, it would cause a huge commotion globally. Muslims all over the world would be protesting and rioting for sure. Atop the Dome of the Rock is a speaker that broadcasts five times a day a call to prayer. Could this be the daily routine that is halted?

One argument against this view is that the Dome of the Rock is not really on the rock of Abraham. A learning center located in a tunnel near the base of the western wall of the temple has some scale models attempting to prove that the crown of mount Zion is a few hundred yards away from the Muslim Dome. The Jews believe and teach that the rock would have been on the very crown of this hill. We don't know for sure whether the Dome of the Rock sits on the altar of Abraham or if there is another rock farther up the hill or if the hill ascends at all because the rest of the Temple Mount is buried under its current platform. Excavation is not allowed because the Temple Mount is controlled by the Muslims. Therefore, I conclude that it is possible that the "holy place" where Abraham offered Isaac could be in the Muslim shrine.

IT'S POSSIBLE

My point here is not to argue for sure that this is how the Abomination of Desolation will happen. I merely want to point out that the idea of a rebuilt temple, which has become so deeply embedded in the mind of the Church, is not as irrefutable as many have thought. Other possibilities exist. Albeit unpopular, this is still a plausible, biblically- consistent option. Like many other historical end-time views, the ideas surrounding the Abomination of Desolation and the rebuilt temple are under scrutiny in these days.

In fact, an entire movement of end-time study is re-examining many of the long-held assumptions about who the Beast and False Prophet are and from where they will come.6 According to this group, the campaign of the Beast and the False Prophet will be an attempt to bring the entire world under the control of Islam—culminating in a turn against the Muslim world and an enactment of the Abomination of Desolation in their holy place. Islam is one of the few world religions that controls even the finances, which is a hallmark event in Revelation 13.

Speaking of the leader of the Beast nations of the last days, Daniel wrote: *Then the king shall do according to his own will: he shall exalt and magnify himself above every god, shall **speak blasphemies against the God of gods,** and shall prosper till the wrath has been accomplished; for what has been determined shall be done. He shall **regard neither the God of his fathers** nor the desire of women, nor regard any god; for he shall exalt himself above them all* (Daniel 11:36–37).

Here it says he will speak blasphemies against the *"God of gods"* as well as refusing to regard *"the God of his fathers."* The God of gods is, of course, the God of the Bible, but who is this *"God of his fathers"*? I find it hard to believe the passage would make such a distinction between the two if, in fact, they were the same God. Rather, I believe this second phrase refers to the god of the religion of the person who commits the Abomination of Desolation—perhaps Allah of the Muslims. According to this theory, the future False Prophet could be a Muslim who erects an idol of some kind in the Dome of the Rock and technically fulfills the prophecy called the Abomination of Desolation. It's possible. I am not attempting to make a solid case that Islam is the Beast of Revelation but simply to establish that the event may or may not happen the way popular eschatology says it will.

WHAT ARE WE BUILDING?

I recall many years ago my pastor teaching that once the European Union reaches twelve nations it will qualify as the Beast of the antichrist. Right now, the European Union has twenty-seven members; clearly, my pastor's theory was misled. Unfortunately, because he preached it like a fact, it misled many others as well. Similarly, in the early '80s, while I was attending a large evangelistic outreach, the guest speaker held up a credit card he had received in the mail that day. The first three numbers of the card were 666. He went on to scare the hell out of everybody by saying that the economic system of the antichrist was already being implemented. The altar call was huge that night. Yet these years later, we all know that preacher's message was based on a false premise. Credit cards and debit cards have become our primary method of payment, and they have nothing to do with the end-times. Similarly, the insistence on the need for a reconstructed temple could end up on the trash heap of bad eschatology.

Unfortunately, so much emphasis has been placed on the reconstruction of the temple as a sign of the times that it is becoming obsessive and distracting for many. Thus I offer this alternative, not as a closed case but as proof that none of us knows with certainty how it'll play out. It is possible that this temple rebuilding may not happen until the world is deep into the Great Tribulation or until after Christ returns. Both of these scenarios would make the temple a moot point in the current Church's end-time strategy. Further, the book of Revelation, if read as a stand-alone prophecy, says nothing about an antichrist person entering into a temple on Temple Mount. It's just not there. I'm not saying it can't or won't happen; I'm just asking that we admit we don't know and stop using hot topic scare tactics to gain attention for the Kingdom. It's just not right. It undermines the Church's goal, credibility, and reputation to the world.

The truth is, I have yet to read an end-times position that didn't have some holes in it, including my own. Here's what I believe: God's Spirit will be poured out on the entire Earth and the next massive harvest of new believers may come from the Jews and Muslims. If that is the case, I doubt these new believers will want a sacrificial temple rebuilt. That would be contradictory to their conversion. As Christians who cherish the value of the once and for all sacrifice Jesus made upon the cross, we of all people should be opposed to a temple built for sacrificial purposes. Certainly God does not want to renew the sacrificial system when Jesus already paid the ultimate sacrifice:

And every priest stands ministering daily and offering repeatedly the same sacrifices, wich can never take away sins. But this Man, after He had offered one sacrifice for sins forever, sat down at the right hand of God, from that time waiting till His enemies are made His footstool. For by one offering He has perfected forever those who are being sanctified (Hebrews 10:11–14).

WHAT I DO KNOW

I've talked a lot about what we don't know for sure. When it comes to end-times prophecy, so much of it is filled with mystery. Fortunately, there are some pieces that seem pretty clear. I believe in an abomination of desolation and a new temple. These are givens, but the timeline of these events—in history or in the future—are not clear. I also know that Jesus warned people (His present listeners and His future readers) to flee Judea when the Abomination of Desolation happens and that He seemed to connect it with His Final Return. On anything more specific than that, I haven't heard a convincing argument from anyone. And I have read and listened to a lot of teaching on this subject. During the sixteen years I spent as a Calvary Chapel pastor, this subject was one of my specialties, as it was for most of my pastoral peers.

I speak from experience when I say it is good to study these things and peer into the window of prophecy, but we must refrain from anything that distracts us from the task at hand. Without a doubt, we are living in an era of Kingdom expansion, Holy Spirit outpouring, and escalating apostolic supernatural power. We are about to reap the greatest harvest for God's Kingdom in all of history. This is our task at hand and our primary focus. Once we've accomplished it, *then* Jesus will return. In the meantime, we must focus on building a Kingdom, not a temple.

Our mandate is not to know all the answers but to spread encounters with God's presence all over the Earth. It is OK to admit that we are waiting for more information or that we aren't sure what the answers are. I am comfortable doing so because my position in Christ is not connected to a temple built for the antichrist to defile— or any other piece of the end-times puzzle. Rather, my position in Christ is rooted in who I am as a child of God and as an ambassador of the ever- increasing Kingdom. However, I do look forward to the day when I will worship Jesus Christ on Mount Zion in His Holy Temple, as the psalmist so eloquently described:

They have seen Your procession, O God, The procession of my God, my King, into the sanctuary. The singers went before, the players on instruments followed after; among them were the maidens playing timbrels. Bless God in the congregations, the Lord, from the fountain of Israel. There is little Benjamin, their leader, the princes of Judah and their company, the princes of Zebulun and the princes of Naphtali. Your God has commanded your strength; strengthen, O God, what You have done for us. Because of Your temple at Jerusalem, kings will bring presents to You. Rebuke the beasts of the reeds, the herd of bulls with the calves of the peoples, till everyone submits himself with pieces of silver. Scatter the peoples who delight in war. Envoys will come out of Egypt; Ethiopia will quickly stretch out her hands to God. Sing to God, you kingdoms of the earth; oh, sing praises to the Lord, Selah (Psalm 68:24–32)

65

4. The Glory Invasion

At this point, I could make a strong case that, from the unbeliever's view, Christianity's message to the world is: "The world is ending, and you are going to hell!" However, I believe God would have us lift our eyes in search of the coming heavenly visitation instead. So many believers have never considered the possibility of a pre-millennium, pre-Rapture global revival that includes the nation of Israel with a huge influx into the Kingdom of Jesus from the Muslim world. It's never occurred to them that revival could start in the Middle East and sweep the entire globe. So many of us, fearful of the end-times, see the Middle East as a threat, and it's understandable, because as of now, they are. However, for the sake of my goal in this chapter, I want us to consider the Middle East as the potential epicenter for the next big move of God. Rather than using our imaginations to ignite fear, let's use them to inspire hope.

For example, consider the possibility of a manifestation of God's presence that is so strong, so powerful, and so visible that the world actually sees it. Imagine what it might look like if the prophecy from Joel, which Peter quoted in Acts 2, has yet to be fulfilled in its entirety— but will be soon.

But this is what was spoken by the prophet Joel: "And it shall come to pass in the last days, says God, that I will pour out My

Spirit on all flesh; your sons and your daughters shall prophesy, your young men shall see visions, your old men shall dream dreams. And on My menservants and on My maidservants I will pour out My Spirit in those days; and they shall prophesy. I will show wonders in heaven above and signs in the earth beneath: blood and fire and vapor of smoke. The sun shall be turned into darkness, and the moon into blood, before the coming of the great and awesome day of the LORD. And it shall come to pass that whoever calls on the name of the LORD shall be saved" (Acts 2:16–21).

Peter certainly identified the fact that the Acts 2 event was a Holy Spirit outpouring; however, we can see that the scope and magnitude that Joel spoke of were not matched on the day of Pentecost in Acts 2. Joel's prophecy is far grander. He wrote *"...I will pour out my Spirit on all flesh..."* (Joel 2:28). The upper room held 120 people. That doesn't qualify as all flesh.

In fact, technically Peter misquoted Joel. Joel said, *"And it shall come to pass **afterward** that I will pour out My Spirit on all flesh..."* (Joel 2:28). The question is, after what? Since Joel 2 is a play-by-play account of the triumphant return of Jesus Christ, we can find our answer simply enough in Joel 2:1–27. In these verses, God promises that—after Christ returns and, with His supernatural army, retakes the Earth—immediately He will pour out His Holy Spirit, and all survivors who call on His name will be saved. So in essence Peter was right. What happened in Acts 2 was a taste of what is to come, but it was not the culmination. I believe it is time for another taste. In Acts 2, 120 people waited on the Lord. Now, millions of Christians around the globe await His visitation! Imagine what it would look like if the entire Church experienced a dose from Heaven today, all at the same time. Or even all within the same week. Imagine what would happen if upper room encounters spread around the globe like wildfires. This is not just speculation; it is God's desire for us. The testimonies of random Jesus visitations are common today. The world is already being touched by the presence of God in unique and undeniable ways.

A friend of mine named Alex Vargas visited Venezuela in 2011. While he was preaching in a small village, many people were healed, and the local witchdoctor received Jesus Christ into his heart. The entire group of about forty people met along a riverbank for a baptism. As the people were gathering, the children climbed the mango trees that provided shade for the group and attempted to knock the mangos from the trees. However, the mangos weren't ripe yet, and the children weren't able to shake them loose or pull them down, so they gave up. The baptism took place, in which the witchdoctor and his elders were baptized, and more people were healed and touched by the presence of God. They closed the gathering with a time of prayer and rejoicing.

Then suddenly something amazing happened. The mangos that the children had previously been unable to pluck from the trees instantly ripened and began to fall on the ground on their own, without being touched. According to Alex, everyone went away rejoicing, healed, born again, and carrying armloads of ripe mangos. What happened? Heaven touched down to Earth. The very atmosphere around them shifted. God intervened, and the blessings of God became available to be had by all.

The Expectant Church

As I mentioned before, I believe Jesus will not return until the Church steps into her full identity and destiny—worldwide Kingdom influence. I also believe the Church needs proactive help from Heaven to get there, because the Church we see and know globally is nowhere near what we all are hoping for. The cry of the Church today is for God to come and for the Holy Spirit to fall. I have witnessed this first hand around the world. Even in the churches who are opposed to what I am proposing, I know for a fact that the people under their leadership are crying out for more. For this reason, I believe we are at the threshold of an unprecedented manifestation of Heaven and visitation by the presence of God. God sees both our weakness and our hunger, and He will not abandon us.

Isaiah 66:9, *"Would I ever bring this nation to the point of birth and then not deliver it?' asks the Lord. 'No! I would never keep this nation from being born,' says your God"* (NLT).

This is God's heart for us. When it comes to the nation of Israel and the Church, God will not impregnate a people with hopes and dreams to the point of labor and then not deliver. I believe that—at a time in the future—the Lord is going to have twins: A revived global Church and a manifestation of His presence in the Middle East that starts in Israel, thus a reborn nation.

In November 2012, I had an unusual experience while preaching at the Meridian Idaho Vineyard. As the evening developed, the Holy Spirit began to move freely in the room, and there was an outbreak of laughter and joy, which is not uncommon. What happened next was. Suddenly five women in the church—within just seconds of each other—began to travail with labor-like sounds and breathing. They were all on the ground at the same time. It wasn't a planned thing, and I don't believe any of them were aware that others were doing the same thing. Clearly, the Holy Spirit had orchestrated it all. As I watched, the Holy Spirit told me that it was a sign of what's coming. Truly, we are nearing the dawn of a great move of God. But here I believe is the key: Look eastward toward Israel. Look to the land where it all began. The Lord will do it again.

A DOSE OF HEAVEN

Right now we are witnessing tumult in the Middle East. As I write, civil war is breaking out in Egypt as the Muslim Brotherhood seems to be plying for dominance. The people are in the streets, and bloodshed is happening all over. Syria is experiencing the same unrest, and the rocket launches from Gaza into Israel by Hamas have escalated the tension in the entire region. But something good is going to happen, and I believe it will happen very soon. I believe God is going to intervene, but before I get to that, I want to look at the Bible's prophecies concerning Egypt. First, please read the entire chapter of Isaiah 19.

The chapter starts off by saying, *"The Lord is advancing against Egypt"* (Isa. 19:1 NLT). In verse two we read, *"I will make Egyptian fight against Egyptian, brother against brother, neighbor against neighbor, city against city, province against province"* (NLT). Considering the current tumult in Egypt, it appears that we may be witnessing the events of Isaiah 19 right now. How long this scenario will last is anybody's guess, but notice the end result:

> *In that day there will be an altar to the Lord in the heart of Egypt, there will be a monument to the Lord at its border. ... The Lord will make Himself known to the Egyptians.... The Lord will strike Egypt, and then he will bring healing. In that day Egypt and Assyria will be connected by a highway. The Egyptians and Assyrians will move freely between their lands, and they will both worship God. And Israel will be their ally...* (Isaiah 19:19,21–24 NLT).

What an amazing prophecy! This is not a Millennium (after Christ returns) event because, if Christ had already returned, Egypt and Assyria would not need an ally. No, this is a future event that will

71

happen prior to Christ's return. This amazing prophecy stirs my imagination and causes me to wonder how this might happen.

There is also a prophetic promise that Iran will also be saved prior to Christ's return. In the following text, Elam is modern-day Iran.

The word of the LORD that came to Jeremiah the prophet against Elam, in the beginning of the reign of Zedekiah king of Judah, saying, "Thus says the LORD of hosts: 'Behold, I will break the bow of Elam, the foremost of their might. Against Elam I will bring the four winds from the four quarters of heaven, and scatter them toward all those winds; there shall be no nations where the outcasts of Elam will not go. For I will cause Elam to be dismayed before their enemies and before those who seek their life. I will bring disaster upon them, My fierce anger,' says the LORD; 'And I will send the sword after them until I have consumed them. I will set My throne in Elam, and will destroy from there the king and the princes,' says the LORD. 'But it shall come to pass in the latter days: I will bring back the captives of Elam,' says the LORD" (Jeremiah 49:34–39).

In summary, this passage tells us that God is going to come against the "bow" of Iran and cause them to be scattered around the world. But after God personally deals with Iran, He will restore them. He says, *"I will set My throne in Elam,"* and, *"I will bring back the captives of Elam."* All of this will happen in the *"latter days."*

This is why I'm convinced that the Church is not going to be raptured any time soon. We don't want to miss the global revival, do we? As I write this book, all of these nations currently pose a huge threat to the security of Israel. But God says that they are going to be saved in the latter days. What could possibly take place that would cause this kind of drastic turn around in the relationship between

Israel and its surrounding jihadist neighbors, who are, at this moment, dire enemies? Digging farther into Scripture provides some answers.

Isaiah 64:1 contains an interesting prayer: *"Oh that You would burst from the heavens and come down! How the mountains would quake in your presence"* (NLT). Based on this, and other texts that we will draw from in this chapter, I believe a coming phenomenon of the manifest presence of God will be witnessed and then experienced by the entire world. I'm not talking about another incarnation but a glorious God event that won't be classified as a *sign from* Heaven but rather as a *dose of* Heaven. It will go way beyond a sign; it will be a chunk of Heaven itself—preceding the Rapture, the Tribulation, and the coming of Jesus. This event will cause the Church's anointing to rise to an unprecedented level. We will explode with confidence and boldness, and the world will cry out for salvation, healing, and help from Jesus. Many throughout the Middle East will be saved, too, as the Spirit of God hits them in full force. Many will actually see the face of God and live.

HEAVEN IS LEAKING NOW

In fall 2010, I had a dream that I was hanging from a scaffold on Shasta dam. Leaks were springing all over the dam, and I was trying my best to repair them. Then I realized it was supposed to happen, and I stopped fixing and started helping the leaks by using tools to chisel open the cracks. A friend of mine was below on the ground hoisting up more tools as I called for certain hammers and spikes and such. All of a sudden, the dam burst. I was being washed down the river, tossed and turned at every curve, and I loved it. I knew in the dream that it was representative of God's Spirit being poured out on the Earth, and there I was right in the midst of it.

Already, hints of Heaven are leaking out on the Earth. The most dramatic that I have seen thus far is the glory cloud of golden, sparkly dust that has been hovering in the sanctuary of Bethel Church in Redding, California, during 2011 and 2012. Sometimes it is small and almost indiscernible; at other times it hovers out over the entire room and is seen by everyone and even captured on video.1 The cloud always seems to be responding to the praise and worship of the church, and the result of its appearance is increased reverence, joy, and praise among the people. To my knowledge and as far as I have personally witnessed, it has never distracted from the worship of God but has rather enhanced it to almost the realm of heavenly encounters. Certainly, it has distracted various Bethel pastors from giving their sermons, but really, when God's in the house, who needs a sermon? I cant prove that the debris was actually from heaven, but I'm convinced that it was initiated by God. No doubt supernatural.

One night in particular stands out to me. The cloud was consuming the entire room so I texted my kids to come. My daughter, Kristen, and her husband, Brandon, showed up with their three kids—Josie (eight years old), Cru (six years old), and Sid (three years old). We all worshipped together, the kids standing on the chairs with their little hands lifted toward Heaven. As I peered down the row, I saw my granddaughter Josie worshipping her God with tears streaming down her cheeks. It hit me at that point that the next big move of God is going to be some kind of visitation or global manifestation of His presence— something that touches the entire globe at the same time.

One afternoon, I was at another church in Redding, The Stirring, where I was hosting an outreach with a metal core band called Sleeping Giant. Prior to the show, we gathered for prayer at the edge of the venue stage. As the twelve of us were praying, I heard a fluttering sound. I looked up and saw a huge cloud of silver confetti-like debris hovering over us. Much of the debris was about a fourth of an inch thick, and the fluttering noise was the sound of the debris brushing against itself. This wasn't just something I saw, but *all* of us saw it! I explained to the group that it was a manifestation sent by the Lord to encourage us. After we finished praying, it disappeared. That night, many people gave their lives to Christ and many were healed. I discovered later that much of the healing happened as the music played, without any healing prayers. The entire room was filled with the presence of God, and sickness and infirmity had to leave.

One Tuesday evening in my home we were hosting a home, Bible study group called Firestarters.2 About fourteen people were present, and the topic for the evening in our workbook was titled "The Glory." That day also happened to be my birthday. After our discussion on the glory of God, someone came out of the kitchen carrying a birthday cake, and everyone started singing "Happy Birthday." I was so honored. As they sang, my wife, Doreen, drew our attention to the ceiling near the wall above our television. A glory cloud filled with tiny feathers and gold sparkly dust hovered in our living room for about twenty minutes. It was incredible! On my birthday, in my home, during a gathering focused on His glory, a cloud of God's presence came into the room. It was the happiest birthday I've ever had. The little group exploded with joy, laughter, and praise. Some were laid out on the chairs and couches while others stood under the cloud and worshipped.

The following prophecy, which the Lord gave me on March 16, 2011, at 11:30 p.m., speaks of what all these hints of Heaven are leading up to. I have cut and pasted it from my iPhone note pad exactly as it was written:

There is a coming move of God that will not be hemmed in or defined by format, facility, or creed. This move will not have a calendar dictated by holidays or tradition.

The coming movement will be recognized solely by supernatural evidences—the presence of angels, the healing of all who come—and the declaration of the Word will be in power and demonstration.

The next harvest of souls will not stand for dry religion in controlled atmospheres kept by well-meaning but powerless stewards of the past forms.

Their gatherings will be unscheduled, spontaneous outpourings in various locations around the city. No one will know when the next corporate gathering is. It will happen so fast with so much power that you will become like storm chasers. It will be in the tradition of Jesus's first ministry. You may have to drive twenty minutes. Simultaneous outbreaks of love, healing, and benevolence will be scattered across the land. Worshippers will gather fast. And so will the lost, sick, and tormented.

My presence will shake the Earth without collateral damage. People will fear but not be hurt. This will be a summons to Me. Text and Twitter and email will play a key role in spreading the news from outpouring to outpouring.

Sabbath will be a day of rest and staying home with the family. Between work and multiple open Heaven outpourings during the week, you will be too tired for "church."

The apostolic ministry and offices of course will remain intact but will spend most of their time dealing with the aftermath of these open Heaven visitations. More like newscasters, just like the first apostles, they will be preaching of all that they've seen and heard. The day is coming when the average believer will say, "We are not following cunningly devised fables; we are eyewitnesses of His majesty."

You asked for more; you're going to get more, but things will be different. Don't pack your bags. You're not coming home yet. In due season. Don't forget that I am not willing that any should perish, and I take no pleasure in the death of the wicked. Sooner than you think, these things will be.

I read this publically for the first time at a church I was peaking at on November, 2012. After the service, the pastor and his wife told me that She had previously had a dream in which she was driving in her car and her text messages were filling up with friends telling her to come to where they were because God was *showing up*. I was so encouraged to hear that others are also hearing from God about the coming visitation. I believe these prophetic experiences will only increase as we get closer to the time when the glory of the Lord is going to cover the Earth (literally!) and cause an influx into the Kingdom of God like never before. This will happen *before* the Rapture so the Lord of the harvest will get His full reward. Contrary to popular opinion, the raptured Church is *not* going to be small and weak. It is preposterous to think that the great harvest that God has been planning for the end of this age will result in only a minuscule minority of over-comers. No way! Our God is much bigger and better than that!

THE GLORY INVASION

What will this *possible* coming visitation that sparks global revival look like? I believe it has to be a global event that is witnessed by most if not all of the world. It will be something so big that it causes the whole world to take notice at the same time. The following is *my theory*— supported by Scripture, of course—of how things *might* *happen.*

ISRAEL FIRST: THE KEY IN EZEKIEL 38–39

One of the keys to understanding the ways of God is understanding His relationship with the Jews and the nation of Israel. This applies to all matters of theology, including eschatology. With this in mind, as I consider the possibility of a global revival that impacts every tribe, tongue, and nation and brings in a massive harvest of souls to the Kingdom of God prior to the Rapture, I believe the nucleus of this revival will be the land of Israel. From there, it will quickly spread— within days—around the globe.

I propose that God is going to trigger, seemingly in a moment, a full-blown outpouring of His Spirit with some kind of manifestation of His presence on the entire world. The yield of this harvest will be so high that it will take every single believer alive at that moment to help teach, disciple, and encourage all the new believers. I am looking for a visitation of God that will induce the birth of global revival, and I believe Israel, Iran, Egypt, and Assyria will be at the epicenter of it all.

Let me explain. In 1990, the United States entered into the Gulf War, leading a coalition of UN forces. The objective was to liberate Kuwait from the attempted overthrow and annexation by Iraq under the infamous and now deceased Saddam Hussein. The initial launch of this campaign was nationally televised. Many Americans watched on CNN or FOX as the United States bombed Baghdad while Baghdad shot up random missiles in a meager attempt to shoot down the U.S. war planes. The campaign was labeled Operation Desert Storm.

That same week, I attended a packed house gathering at Calvary Chapel Costa Mesa and listened to a sermon telling tell us that this may be the beginnings of Ezekiel 38. These years later, we know it wasn't that at all. This shows how easily even legitimate experts on end-time Bible prophecy can jump to conclusions, and this also proves that the timing of Ezekiel 38 is uncertain, even for some of the most diligent chart-setting, sequence-offering Bible teachers. Many end- times teachers say that Ezekiel 38–39 will happen after the Rapture during the Great Tribulation. Others say it will happen before. Both camps usually qualify their positions with the admission that this event sequence is ambiguous. Thus, they intensely attempt to prove that their particular understanding is correct.

I recently watched a world-renowned end-times scholar on GodTV say that the Ezekiel 38–39 scenario has to happen after the Tribulation because there is no way God would reveal Himself so personally and powerfully on Israel's behalf prior to it. This grieved my heart because, in essence, this excellent Bible teacher has lost hope for a global God encounter and for the salvation of the Jews prior to the Rapture. That is eschatological defeatism at its finest—or should I say *worst*.

I am convinced that the events of Ezekiel 38 are up for grabs and are fair game for positioning. I also believe they are key to this glorious revival end-time sequence. (If anyone wants to destroy my theory, this is good place to do it. But first, such people will have to prove beyond doubt that the events of Ezekiel 38–39 have already happened or that they will not happen until after the Church is raptured.) Let's take a closer look.

In Ezekiel 38–39, the Bible prophesies a time when the nation of Israel will be under attack by surrounding nations. Included on the list of nations that will come against Israel are Iran, Libya, and Egypt (see Ezek. 38:5), along with many others. In this passage, Ezekiel described in detail a huge and overwhelming coalition of nations that will *"ascend, coming like a storm, covering the land like a cloud..."* (Ezek. 38:9). Unfortunately for them, they will not succeed because God Himself will intervene.

As I write this chapter, Israel is under attack by Hamas from the Gaza strip. They are shooting missiles at Tel Aviv and Jerusalem, and Israel's defense minister has called for 75,000 troops to be ready. Egypt is getting into the fray, and Iran, who supports Hamas financially, has been habitually threatening to wipe Israel off the face of the Earth. Several months ago, on September 11, 2012, Libyan terrorists attacked the United States Embassy in Bengazi and murdered our ambassador, J. Christopher Stevens, and three others. Syria is in a full-scale civil war, and Lebanon has been firing rockets into Israel. All of these nations are listed in Ezekiel 38 as part of a coalition that will come against Israel.

The following four verses, taken from the same chapter that describes this invasion, are God's direct response to the situation:

...My fury will show in My face. For in My jealousy and in the fire of My wrath I have spoken: "Surely in that day there shall be a great earthquake in the land of Israel." ...Thus I will magnify Myself and sanctify Myself, and **I will be known in the eyes of many nations...** (Ezekiel 38:18–19, 23).

When God said, *"I will be known in the eyes of many nations,"* He pronounced a clear, non-ambiguous promise to let Himself be seen visibly in the eyes of many nations. The promises of the next chapter are even better:

So I will make My Holy Name known in the midst of My people Israel, and I will not let them profane My holy name anymore.

*Then **the nations will know that I am the Lord, the Holy One in Israel** (Ezekiel 39:7).*

*I will set My glory among the nations: **all the nations shall see** my judgment which I have executed, and My hand which I have laid on them. So the house of **Israel shall know that I am the Lord their God from that day forward** (Ezekiel 39:21–22).*

*And **I will not hide My face from them anymore;** for I shall have **poured out My Spirit on the house of Israel,** says the Lord God (Ezekiel 39:29).*

This is incredible. When the nation of Israel is about to be or is in the midst of an attack by a massive coalition of surrounding nations (all of which are Muslim), God Himself is going to intervene in a way that will be witnessed *"in the eyes of many nations,"* resulting in the nations acknowledging the Lord, Israel acknowledging the Lord as their God, and God pouring out His Spirit on Israel.

In my opinion, this event in Ezekiel 38–39 is a full-blown, visible manifestation of the presence of God over the nation of Israel. Ezekiel 38:23 clearly states that this manifestation of God will be visibly seen by the rest of world. From then on, the veil of blindness will be lifted from Israel and, consequently, from the entire world. This will set the stage for what we have all been praying for—souls and more souls. The following verses from the book of Psalms also speak into this prophecy. The following Psalm may even be in direct reference to the Ezekiel 38 events:

In my distress I called upon the LORD, and cried out to my God; He heard my voice from His temple, and my cry came before Him, even to His ears. Then the earth shook and trembled; the foundations of the hills also quaked and were shaken, because He was angry. Smoke went up from His nostrils, and devouring fire from His mouth; coals were kindled by it. **He bowed the heavens also, and came down with darkness under His feet.** *And He rode upon a cherub, and flew; He flew upon the wings of the wind. He made darkness His secret place; His canopy around Him was dark waters and thick clouds of the skies. From the brightness before Him, His thick clouds passed with hailstones and coals of fire. The LORD thundered from heaven, and the Most High uttered His voice, hailstones and coals of fire. He sent out His arrows and scattered the foe, lightnings in abundance, and He vanquished them. Then the channels of the sea were seen, the foundations of the world were uncovered at Your rebuke, O LORD, at the blast of the breath of Your nostrils. He sent from above, He took me; He drew me out of many waters.* **He delivered me from my strong enemy, from those who hated me, for they were too strong for me.** *They confronted me in the day of my calamity, but the LORD was my support. He also brought me out into a broad place; He delivered me because He delighted in me* (Psalm 18:6–19).

...THEN THE WORLD

This intervention of God's presence will be a treacherous event for the attacking armies against Israel, but it will also be a glorious event for the rest of the world. Why? Because at the same time God manifests on behalf of Israel, He also promises to set His glory among the nations (see Ezek. 39:21).

Consider the possibility that, when the Muslim nations that currently surround Israel finally do attempt to destroy it, the very events that Satan meant for bad, God will use for good. God will respond with a massive, visible display of His power and His presence over the nation of Israel. The whole world will see, and the Jews will immediately experience an outpouring of the Holy Spirit that will never fade from that day forward. As Ezekiel prophesied,

"And I will not hide my face from them anymore; for I shall have poured out My Spirit on the house of Israel, says the Lord God" (Ezek. 39:29).

In a matter of days, that same Holy Spirit outpouring will spread over the entire Muslim world. Israel's surrounding enemies will abandon their post, and those who aren't killed by the presence of God will walk away from their artillery in fear of almighty God. It will take seven years to gather and recycle all the hardware lying around. Perhaps the materials from this massive recycling process will even be used to manufacture farming equipment to facilitate the massive effort by the multi-billion soul harvest to feed the world.

Notice Ezekiel 39:9: *Then those who dwell in the cities of Israel will go out and set on fire and burn the weapons; both the shields and the bucklers, the bows and arrows, the javelins and spears; and they will make fires with them for seven years.*

This massive display of God's power and presence will reverberate around the entire globe, and people from every tribe, tongue, and nation will be drawn to the God of Israel and their Messiah, Jesus Christ. The entire Earth will be filled with the glory of God as the residue of His manifestation over Israel spreads. God's Ezekiel 38 intervention will be globally visible via television, YouTube, social media, and smart phone videos, and the whole world will see the mighty power of God displayed on behalf of His people. People will be flocking to churches that have been marked by the glory. Is it possible that this is the prophecy Paul spoke of in Romans 8:19, *"For the earnest expectation of the creation eagerly waits for the revealing of the sons of God"?* Denominationalism will be eradicated. The Church will simply be marked by His glory. Our gatherings will "glow in the dark."

THE HISTORY OF MORE

In the book of Acts, Peter and John were arrested, persecuted, and put on trial for healing a lame man at the gate beautiful. Upon release, they returned to the place where all their friends were hanging out, and they shared the story of what had happened. The response was a corporate plea for God to grant them more boldness in order to continue sharing the gospel. And God responded powerfully:

Now, Lord, look on their threats, and grant to Your servants that with all boldness they may speak Your word, by stretching out Your hand to heal, and that signs and wonders may be done through the name of Your holy Servant Jesus."

And when they had prayed, the place where they were assembled together was shaken; and they were all filled with the Holy Spirit, and they spoke the word of God with boldness.

Now the multitude of those who believed were of one heart and one soul; neither did anyone say that any of the things he possessed was his own, but they had all things in common. And with great power the apostles gave witness to the resurrection of the Lord Jesus. And great grace was upon them all (Acts 4:29–33).

During that time, the religious, antichrist leaders (antichrist means "anti-anointed") were attempting to minimize the effectiveness of the apostles' supernatural ministry. In return, the Church cried out to God for more. God responded with a great shaking that emboldened and empowered the believers. I believe these historical events are a foreshadowing of what is about to happen in our own day.

Today, as we are realizing the power of God to heal, the Church is beginning to cry out to God to prove Himself to the world. I have witnessed the Church, not only in my home, at Bethel Church, but also in various parts of the world, crying out for more. We have pressed in to His presence like never before, and miracles are beginning to abound, but we want more. We are convinced there is more and that God wants us to have more because *"God so loved the world"* that He wants to be known (see John 3:16). He wants full disclosure of His love for humanity, and He has decided that we will be the agents who bring about His change and carry His gospel.

My current eschatology, based on the afore-mentioned Scriptures, leads me to believe that when the nations that hate Israel finally decide to attack them, attempting to destroy them, God is going to intervene on Israel's behalf in a way that will shake the foundations of the world and the Church. Then, just as God promised in Ezekiel 39:29, *"I will not hide my face anymore."* He will release a global version of what He did for the Church in Acts 4:31. The visible manifestation of God's presence will embolden the Church to such a degree that finally the whole world will be impacted by the gospel. It will start with the visible manifestation of God's glory above Israel. The glory will literally spread around the world in a matter of days. Billions of people will be drawn into the Kingdom by miraculous signs and wonders and miracles. Supernatural Christianity will be the only Christianity they know.

This outpouring of His Holy Spirit will manifest in the bodies of men and women in unprecedented ways. Mass healings will break out across Egypt, just like Isaiah prophesied in Isaiah 19:22. The very nation that was stricken by plagues during the Exodus will become a healing revival center. All of the people who scattered from Iran will return, and God's presence will rest in that nation too, which will become a global worship and healing center where we will rejoice together as one people. Throughout the Earth, miracles will be easy and normal. Lame people will walk, blind eyes will open, limbs will grow out—and so forth. This will continue, and the presence of God will remain on the Earth until all who would be saved are saved. Only then, in my opinion, will we be ready for that glorious day when the entire body of Christ ascends into Heaven, bypassing death itself and entering right into the glorious presence of God. From Earth's perspective, this is nothing more than a temporary evacuation for the sake of fumigation.

Unfortunately, instead of anticipating the glory that's coming, much of the Church world is looking for a revived Roman empire and a rebuilt temple, and they are pointing fingers at the Catholic Church or criticizing other church movements they don't understand. All the while, I believe we are nearing the cusp of the biggest outpouring of God's Spirit since Christ rose from the grave. Over the course of just a few days, we may find ourselves in charge of the entire globe, wondering how to feed, heal, disciple, and teach the masses of new converts.

If we want to speculate about what might happen in the near future, we should speculate on the contents of this chapter. At the very least, we should consider the possibilities of this coming visitation.

Here are some of the questions that I've been pondering:

What if God is waiting for the message of His coming visitation to empower the Church with hope so that He can follow through and answer the cry of our hearts for more?

What if God sits in Heaven and is waiting for someone to discover a potential scenario in Scripture for worldwide revival and then have the nerve to ask Him to do it?

What if God wrote the Bible in a way that allows us to help script the future, as if to say, "Here are My non-negotiable, now fill in the blanks"?

This is radical thinking! For me, this is the bottom line: I really want to see the world come to know Jesus! You can consider this chapter either a prophecy or a prayer request. Either way, it's good. I hope you are excited by now! I know I am.

No one lights a lamp and then covers it with a bowl or hides it under a bed. A lamp is placed on a stand, where its light can be seen by all who enter the house. For all that is secret will eventually be brought into the open, and everything that is concealed will be brought to light and made known to all. "So pay attention to how you hear. To those who listen to my teaching, more understanding will be given. But for those who are not listening, even what they think they understand will be taken away from them (Luke 8:16–18 NLT).

5. The Rapture

Simply put, the Rapture can be defined as an event in which the Church is taken from the Earth prior to the end of the world. We've already discussed it at several places in earlier chapters, but here I want to give a more in depth look at what Scripture says and offer an alternative view to most modern views. First, I will summarize the existing views of the Rapture and its timing:

- Some say the Rapture will happen prior to the Great Tribulation (commonly called Pre-Trib).

- Others place the Rapture somewhere in the middle of the Great Tribulation (commonly called Mid-Trib).

- Still others place the Rapture after the Great Tribulation, just prior to Christ's return (commonly called Post-Trib).

- There are even some who dismiss the idea of the Rapture altogether.

There are scholarly approaches to all these views. And let's face it, we are all speculating based on our understanding of Scripture, our beliefs about the Church's role in the world, historical events, and geopolitical conditions today. We are also influenced by our emotional responses to other people's attitudes about and interpretations of the last days. I would never be one to hold other people's eschatology against them, and I hope for the same grace from my readers. Hopefully we can all agree that some huge event globally, internationally, or theologically, could happen tomorrow that would cause every one of us to go back to the drawing board. Nothing proves this better than the rebirth of the nation of Israel in 1947. On that day, to many in the Church, it suddenly seemed as though entire volumes of protestant reformation commentaries on the end-times might as well be thrown in the trash. Great theologians such as Matthew Henry had no grid for a rebirth of the physical nation of Israel. As far as I know, no one did back in the 1700s. Therefore, Matthew Henry spiritualized every prophetic word about Israel's future and attributed these words to the Church. Theories such as his are known today as replacement theology. Though some still hold these views, Messianic Jews—Jews who believe in Jesus as their Messiah—are offended at those teachings and some even see them as anti-Semitic.

My point is this: In a very short period of time, what seemed to be outstanding scholarly interpretations of biblical prophecy about Israel and the last days became obsolete. While it was and is true that many of the dedicated reformed scholars clung to (and still do cling to) those ideas, much of the rest of Christianity moved on to re-examine Scripture in the light of Israel's rebirth as a literal nation. We discovered that the dry bones of Ezekiel can and do live again. I recently heard Benjamin Netanyahu quote that passage in his speech to the world about Israel's rightful place in the land as a nation. It is with this understanding that I write, with trepidation, about my own views.

SEPARATE COMINGS

Having summarized the various views and emphasized the importance of doctrinal humility, I now will explain why I believe the Church will be raptured and why I believe it will happen prior to the Great Tribulation. First on my list of reasons is the following quote from the prophet Isaiah:

> *Awake and sing, you who dwell in dust; for your dew is like the dew of herbs, and the earth shall cast out the dead. Come, my people, enter your chambers, and shut your doors behind you; hide yourself, as it were, for a little moment, until the indignation is past. For behold, the LORD comes out of His place to punish the inhabitants of the earth for their iniquity; the earth will also disclose her blood, and will no more cover her slain* (Isaiah 26:19–21).

Here Isaiah foresaw an event in which the Earth *"casts out her dead"* and the Lord brings His people into a safe place until *"the indignation is past."* To me, this sounds an awful lot like Isaiah saw a prophetic vision of the Rapture prior to the Tribulation.

Second, it's important to understand that, when it comes to the return of Jesus Christ, the Bible seems to describe *two* separate events clearly. Once a critic of mine asked me, "How can there be two second comings?" Logically, there can't. However, this critic failed to realize that the phrase *second coming* is not in the Bible, but is a term the Church adopted to refer to the return of Jesus. In fact, there is no biblical basis for the idea that Jesus will only come one more time. As far as I am concerned, Jesus can come and go as often as He likes. He appeared on the Earth many times during the Old Testament (a pre- incarnate appearance is called a theophany), and He's welcome to do so again. From this, we can logically conclude that the Bible does, in fact, speak of multiple comings.

Here are a couple of examples from Scripture. The two passages both describe the scenario of a coming of the Lord, but they are obviously not the same event:

And if I go and prepare a place for you, I will come again and receive you to Myself; that where I am, there you may be also (John 14:3).

Then the LORD will go forth and fight against those nations, as He fights in the day of battle. And in that day His feet will stand on the Mount of Olives, which faces Jerusalem on the east. And the Mount of Olives shall be split in two, from east to west, making a very large valley; half of the mountain shall move toward the north and half of it toward the south. Then you shall flee through My mountain valley, for the mountain valley shall reach to Azal. Yes, you shall flee as you fled from the earthquake in the days of Uzziah king of Judah. Thus the LORD my God will come, and all the saints with You (Zechariah 14:3–5).

Both of these texts are about Jesus's return. In the first, Jesus clearly explains to His disciples that He will come and receive them to Himself. By contrast, Zechariah's prophecy to Israel describes an event when the Lord will return in defense of Israel, bringing all the saints with Him. Clearly, these two events seem to be separate. One is a gathering of the saints to go be with the Lord, and the other is a dramatic return of the Lord with the saints in tow. I believe the first quote speaks of the Rapture and the second prophesies the final return of Christ.

Let's look at a couple more texts that have similar contrasts:

Now I saw heaven opened, and behold, a white horse. And He who sat on him was called Faithful and True, and in righteousness He judges and makes war. His eyes were like a flame of fire, and on His head were many crowns. He had a name written that no one knew except Himself. He was clothed with a robe dipped in blood, and His name is called The Word of God. And the armies in heaven, clothed in fine linen, white and clean, followed Him on white horses. Now out of His mouth goes a sharp sword, that with it He should strike the nations. And He Himself will rule them with a rod of iron. He Himself treads the winepress of the fierceness and wrath of Almighty God. And He has on His robe and on His thigh a name written: KING OF KINGS AND LORD OF LORDS (Revelation 19:11–16)

Then the kingdom of heaven shall be likened to ten virgins who took their lamps and went out to meet the bridegroom. Now five of them were wise, and five were foolish. Those who were foolish took their lamps and took no oil with them, but the wise took oil in their vessels with their lamps. But while the bridegroom was delayed, they all slumbered and slept. And at midnight a cry was heard: "Behold, the bridegroom is coming; go out to meet him!" Then all those virgins arose and trimmed their lamps. And the foolish said to the wise, "Give us some of your oil, for our lamps are going out." But the wise answered, saying, "No, lest there should not be enough for us and you; but go rather to those who sell, and buy for yourselves." And while they went to buy, the bridegroom came, and those who were ready went in with him to the wedding; and the door was shut. Afterward the other virgins came also, saying, "Lord, Lord, open to us!" But he answered and said, "Assuredly, I say to you, I do not know you." Watch therefore, for you know neither the day nor the hour in which the Son of Man is coming (Matthew 25:1–13).

Once again, we have what appears to be two separate events, yet both are the coming of Jesus Christ. In Revelation, He is in full battle array and ready to *"strike the nations"*; with Him are the *"armies in*

93

heaven, clothed in fine linen, white and clean." On the other hand, in the event described by Jesus in Matthew, He is coming to gather the virgins who are ready to go with Him to the wedding. Once again, He is gathering believers to *go with Him,* in contrast to returning as a conquering King with an army of saints who are *already with Him.*

The Bible contains many more similar comparisons between what appear to be two separate events—the taking away of the saints and the triumphant Final Return of Jesus with the saints. One is a very stealthy and quick event, and the other is a drawn out event that includes the rescue and reclaiming of Israel and Jerusalem. (I speak in much more detail on the triumphant return of Jesus in Chapter 10). I could continue for many pages with proofs for why I believe in these two separate comings, but my intention is not to be exhaustive or comprehensive on the matter. Rather, my overall goal is to lay out an eschatological framework that has a *glorious, victorious, and massive end-time Church* with a harvest numbering in the billions.

THE RAPTURE AS APOSTOLIC TEACHING

Clearly, Scripture provides much backing for the idea of the Rapture, when Jesus comes and takes the Church away with Him prior to His Final Return. First Corinthians 15 gives us more insight on this idea, where the apostle Paul wrote about the resurrection of the dead. In this amazing letter, Paul described the differences between terrestrial and celestial bodies. He also explained how the body dies and is buried like a seed. In the same way that a natural seed is sown into the ground and from it something more glorious bursts forth, so our human bodies die in order to produce heavenly bodies. His overall point in this teaching is that our earthly bodies are not able to translate into the eternal heavenly realm without being transformed supernaturally. He says that the human body is *"sown a natural body"* and *"raised a spiritual body"* (1 Cor. 15:44). His entire

94

emphasis is this translation from flesh to spirit—from a corruptible body to an incorruptible one. In this context, he drops a bomb:

Behold, I tell you a mystery: We shall not all sleep, but we shall all be changed—in a moment, in the twinkling of an eye, at the last trumpet. For the trumpet will sound, and the dead will be raised incorruptible, and we shall be changed. For this corruptible must put on incorruption, and this mortal must put on immortality. So when this corruptible has put on incorruption, and this mortal has put on immortality, then shall be brought to pass the saying that is written: "Death is swallowed up in victory" (1 Corinthians 15:51–54).

In the midst of Paul's revelatory teaching about our victory over the sting of death, he added that not all are going to die, but that all are going to experience a supernatural metamorphosis, *"We shall not all sleep, but we shall all be changed."* Paul called it *"a mystery,"* which Pastor Bill Johnson defines this way: "A mystery is not something hidden *from* us, but *for* us."

In First Corinthians 2:7, Paul wrote, *"We speak the wisdom of God in a mystery, the hidden wisdom which God ordained before the ages for our glory."* The mysteries of God and the revelations delivered to us in the gospels are for our glory and our understanding, for us to search out. The instant translation of some of us from mortal to immortal—literally bypassing death—which is otherwise known as the Rapture, is one of them. It is a glorious mystery.

The idea of a future generation on this Earth that will never taste death is a glorious truth—one to be savored and reminded of. I believe it is going to be one of the final end-time harvests prior to the Great Tribulation. When we think of harvest, we often think in terms of new souls brought into the Kingdom of God. However, the Rapture is actually the harvest. It is a literal gathering of the fruit of Christ's labor unto Himself—just like a ripe field is reaped of the yield that the landowner has been working toward. This event will be God's swansong of human redemption. The greatest single harvest of souls in the history of the universe will be a company of saints that will never die, harvested right from this Earth into Heaven. (Later in this book, I will establish why I believe there will be more than one of this kind of harvest.) As the apostle Paul wrote, *"Then shall be brought to pass the saying that is written: 'Death is swallowed up in victory'"* (1 Cor.15:54). Thus, the mandatory sting of death for all humanity will be overridden before the Final Return of Jesus Christ.

The Church of the last days will not only be a supernatural army of manifest sons and daughters of God. They will not only be able to heal the sick, cast out demons, and raise the dead (to a greater degree than Jesus did), but they will also never have to taste the sting of death. This means that the final revival will be an eternal harvest of souls who have experienced victory over death itself—which is the ultimate healing. What an incredible hope!

Clearly, the doctrine of the Rapture is not an escapist theology when we understand it in its proper context and are willing to rejoice in it for what it really is—an entire generation of believers who have conquered death, thus completely destroying the works of the devil. Not only will Satan not get the satisfaction of hindering their effectiveness on Earth, but he will not even get the satisfaction of watching them die! Far from escapism, this is the ultimate victory, and it is part of God's plan for humanity's future.

Now that I've established the biblical basis and purpose of the Rapture, I want to move on to the reasons why I believe the Rapture will happen *before* the unfolding of the dramatic events described in Revelation 4–22.

THE BREVITY OF THE TRIBULATION

My principal belief that the Lord responds directly to the prayers of His people is one of the reasons why I believe the Church has to be taken out of the way before the final days. By the time this world reaches the end-times, the Church will have come into her full identity. The glory of God will have covered the Earth, and our maturity in the supernatural will have established a very Christ-like Church. For this reason, our very presence on the Earth could have a polarizing affect on the final stages of God's plan to get rid of Satan and his demonic army. The immature Church wants out of here, but a mature Church at the end could be powerful enough to actually get in the way! I believe it's possible that the Church will become so effective at destroying the works of the devil that believers may feel as though they have him on a short enough leash to keep going. With this mindset, it could be tempting to pray that the coming golden era of the Church would be perpetual.

However, even the Church in full-scale revival on its best day is still leavened bread. And even though the Church will be able to effectively spread the gospel over the entire Earth, there will still be pockets of idolatry and people groups who are intent on evil. According to all of the Old Testament prophets, many people will remain unrepentant and hardened, even dabbling in idolatry (see Isa. 2:5–8; Joel 2:12–17; Zech. 13:2–3; Micah 7:18–20; Hosea 14:8; Ezek. 43:8). Thus, it makes sense to me that, for all of the events described in Revelation 6–19 to escalate within such a short time frame, seven years or less, the Church of the last days, mighty and powerful as she is, would need to be out of the way.

LETTERS TO THE CHURCH

With these things in mind, let's look at Christ's letters to the Church in Revelation. The apostle John, while in exile, wrote these seven letters to seven churches, which were dictated to him directly by Jesus. Immediately after John's record of the seven letters to the churches, we read the following:

> *After these things I looked, and behold, a door standing open in heaven. And the first voice which I heard was like a trumpet speaking with me, saying, "Come up here, and I will show you things which must take place **after this"** (Revelation 4:1).*

Here the voice emphasizes that the events that are about to be described *"must take place after this."* I believe this refers to the time after the entire church age has finished our work. These seven letters, filled with both praises and rebukes, are directly from Jesus Christ, who is the head of the Church. They were written to the seven churches of Asia at that time, but they are also all inclusive for the entire Church of all time. From the day the Church was birthed in Acts 2 until the day the Church is caught up to be with the Lord (and then subsequently returns with Jesus, as described in Zechariah 14 and Revelation 19), these letters apply.

Some say these seven letters were specific to the churches of Asia and only apply to us in principal, providing lessons that help us govern the Church today. I understand this reasoning, yet I see in these letters statements that transcend the entire Church age, as if Jesus was speaking to the entire Church age directly through the seven churches of Asia.

For instance, Revelation 3:10–11 says: *Because you have kept My command to persevere, I also will keep you from the hour of trial which shall come upon the whole world, to test those who dwell on the earth. Behold, I am coming quickly...*

Here Jesus spoke of an *"hour of trial which shall come upon the whole world."* The Greek word for world that John used in this quote from Jesus is *oikoumene,* which, according to Strong's Concordance, can mean "the entire inhabited Earth."[1] It is not limited to local interpretation but is in reference to a global experience. Jesus then followed up that statement by saying it is *"to test those who dwell on the earth."* The word for *earth* is *ge,* which is used for local reference, such as "land" or "boundaries," but more specifically, it is used to distinguish between land and sky, or land and sea, or the land of one nation as opposed to another.[2] Thus, I can paraphrase that text as follows while staying well within its intended meaning: *An hour of trial that affects the entire globe to test those who live across the land.*

The obvious intended meaning is global, but in no way was any trial or persecution of the churches in Asia of global consequence. I can't imagine that the events and persecutions of the churches in Asia under the likes of Caesar Nero had any effect whatsoever on the people in China or the South American continent. No doubt, in Revelation 3:10–11, Jesus was referring to something of great consequence that would have impact around the world. In fact, I believe He was referring directly to the events described later on in the book of Revelation, from chapter 6 onward. Those future events will be truly global in scale.

This is just one example from the seven letters that seems to indicate that their application is much broader than just seven churches at that time. With that context in mind, it appears to me that the voice saying to John, *"Come up here, and I will show you things which must take place **after this"*** was referring to what will happen after the Church has completed the mandate to disciple the nations and is removed from the Earth. Thus, the remainder of the book of Revelation, beginning in chapter 4, could happen centuries from now, after the Church has come into her fullness via Gods glory infusion and we have begun operating with great precision and effectiveness in the supernatural.

This discussion does pose an interesting question about the seven letters to the churches. If they are addressed to seven actual churches at the time John transcribed them and they have an intended thrust into the future Church at the time preceding the Rapture, how do we apply them practically today? For those of us who are living in the gap, what do those letters say to us? I believe they provide a clear list from Jesus as to what He admonishes within the Church and what He abhors. I am the youngest of five children. I learned at an early age how to navigate in my family by watching how my parents dealt with my older siblings. This told me what to expect and helped me establish my own principals and boundaries for daily life. This is how I see these letters. One day we will all stand before Christ at an awards ceremony where we will be held accountable for our deeds. We won't be judged in a negative sense, but we will be assessed by our King (see 2 Cor. 5:10; Rom. 14:10). As I once told my congregation, "The seven letters to the seven churches are the answers to the coming exam."

UNDERSTANDING WRATH

Clearly, the Rapture is a bold statement about the quality and kind of victory the Church of the last days will be able to walk in. The idea of this victorious Church having to hang around and endure the day of God's wrath—against Satan and those who have arrogantly and defiantly chosen his kingdom over God's Kingdom—makes no sense to me at all. God's wrath is not against the saints but against the persistently unrighteous, those who refuse to see His goodness even in the midst of His glory outpouring and global revival. Yet by God's goodness, even many of them will be saved in and through the process of the Great Tribulation. Paul clearly spelled out God's intention toward the Church when he wrote:

For God did not appoint us to wrath, but to obtain salvation through our Lord Jesus Christ, who died for us, that whether we wake or sleep, we should live together with Him (1 Thessalonians 5:9–10).

We are not appointed for wrath, but for salvation. It doesn't get any clearer than that. This should not surprise us, however, when we have a revelation of God's heart toward all of humanity. He loves us beyond comprehension, and Revelation clearly indicates that, at the end, even many of the hardest of hearts will turn toward His love during the Great Tribulation.

Over the years, I have heard many sermons and songs and seen movies that depict a day after the Rapture scenario where the churches are all empty and a few sad folks hang around wishing they had received Jesus. I believe that, within a few days after the Rapture, many of those who were left behind will have a change of heart, and a large percentage of people from around the globe will give their lives and hearts to Jesus Christ. They will know the time is short, they will understand what's going on, and they will be filled and overflowing with the Holy Spirit immediately. God's love is so great that He is working very hard to redeem even the most resistant. In the end, we will see that on a greater scale than ever before.

How Soon?

Whenever the topic of the Rapture comes up, people wonder, *How soon will this happen?* The truth is, none of us knows for sure, but

Jesus did give us some signs to follow (see Matt. 24). As I said in Chapter 2, I am convinced in my heart that the Church is not even close (as I write this at the beginning of 2013) to being caught up in the Rapture. For the Lord to remove the Church today, in the midst of revival and a massive movement of healing and miracles around the world, would be detrimental to the very command He has given the Church. This is not in God's best interest. Until the Church is on the other side of a worldwide revival, it is safe to stop thinking about the Rapture in an immediate sense altogether.

When people ask me, "Are we in the last days?" I say yes because we've been in the last days ever since Christ ascended to Heaven. The Bible clearly speaks of the entire New Testament era as the last days: *"Long ago God spoke many times and in many ways to our ancestors through the prophets. And now in **these final days,** he has spoken to us through his Son"* (Heb. 1:1–2). Yet, I doubt the Rapture will happen in my lifetime. But I could be wrong. Perhaps in the next few years we see a massive harvest and the entire Earth will be filled with His glory so that the kingdoms of the Earth become the kingdoms of our God. It is possible that we who are alive today could be in that group of end-time saints who *"in a moment, in the twinkling of an eye"* are caught up to be with the Lord and never have to taste death. Certainly, it is possible. If it is my destiny, I will gladly embrace it, but for now, it must not be my focus.

The mystery of the Rapture must never be a distraction from our commission to disciple the planet. Rather, it should be a motivating force within us that causes us to evangelize our cities and our nations. It should be a motivating force that moves us to grow in our understanding of the supernatural and our ability to perform great miracles in the name of Jesus. Bottom line: If our Rapture eschatology causes us to think of leaving this Earth ASAP, while billions have yet to be shown an authentic gospel, then we are in error.

FORWARD WITH HOPE

It's time for a shift in our perspective. It's time we realign our priorities with Heaven and focus on the task at hand. I believe the following text describes the era we are currently living in:

> Jesus said to them, "My food is to do the will of Him who sent Me, and to finish His work. Do you not say, 'There are still four months and then comes the harvest'? Behold, I say to you, lift up your eyes and look at the fields, for they are already white for harvest (John 4:34–35).

We are entering one of the most incredible seasons of Church history! It is a season of reaping and manifold harvest. It is also a season of hope. I know many who hope for the coming visitation yet want nothing to do with talk of the Rapture. I believe we must have both; together they birth in us the fullness of hope.

I am not ready to ditch the idea of the Rapture just because some have zealously over-hoped for it. And the alternative theories are very weak in my estimation. One of the biggest errors of the Jesus People movement was an over-correction of the errors of the prior Pentecostal movement. The work and ministry of the Holy Spirit were shoved into a back room, so He left. It is possible to make the same mistake by being critical of the Rapture doctrine because of the ways it's been exploited and misunderstood—even though it is a wonderful mystery of God's plan. By our very words and actions, we can cause an entire generation of believers to lose out on the joy of a beautiful hope, the churches corporate victory and destruction of the sting of death. Then in that void create an eschatology to replace it, thus downgrading our future hope.

103

As we diligently work for the harvest, the Rapture should serve as our hallmark goal and hope—not for escape but for the ultimate victory. Consider the reality that those we lay hands on and heal or deliver could possibly be the first fruits of an entire group of believers who will not only walk in divine health, but will never even die! They may be the generation that becomes so effective in reaching the world that they become participants of Jesus's intervention. When He steps down from His throne and welcomes an entire company of people into their eternal destinies—an entire company of people who were harvested from the Earth without knowing the sting of death—those we ministered to may be among their number.

Or maybe we will even be among that number! If my Ezekiel 38 theory is correct, and if it were to happen soon, then our generation could become such a powerful presentation of the gospel that all who would be saved will be saved. This, in turn, would invite Jesus to claim His full reward, turning the page of future events and moving on to the next chapter—the extermination of Satan and his demonic forces from the Earth. The apostle Paul recognized, this is our great hope and comfort:

> *For this we say to you by the word of the Lord, that we who are alive and remain until the coming of the Lord will by no means precede those who are asleep. For the Lord Himself will descend from heaven with a shout, with the voice of an archangel, and with the trumpet of God. And the dead in Christ will rise first. Then we who are alive and remain shall be caught up together with them in the clouds to meet the Lord in the air. And thus we shall always be with the Lord.* **Therefore comfort one another with these words** *(1 Thessalonians 4:15–18).*

PART 2
A UNIQUE VIEW OF THE BOOK OF REVELATION

INTRODUCTION

Of Cosmic Proportions

The second part of this book deals with one of the most elusive and debated books of the entire Bible—the book of Revelation. No small debate rages regarding the historicity of the book and the future of it. I could go on and on listing the quandary of thoughts and speculations about this heavily discussed and documented series of events. Having researched the various views, such as preterism, partial-preterism, pre-millennialism, a-millennialism, post-millennialism, futurism, and so forth, I have taken the position that the events we are about to examine will happen in the future.

The following statement by Jesus makes it clear that the there will be a period of great tribulation, unprecedented in scope and magnitude, that will never be matched again. That alone tells me that all of the events that have happened to date—which may seem to fulfill the events described in Revelation—are not in totality what Jesus was referring to when He said: *"For then there will be great tribulation, such as has not been since the beginning of the world until this time, no, nor ever shall be"* (Matt. 24:21).

When Jesus referred to the world, He used the word *kosmos,* in essence indicating, "There will be great tribulation, such has not been seen since the beginning of the universe." Jesus made such an extreme statement because the events of Revelation will not only impact humanity and the Earth we live on, but also the terrestrial bodies around us—the sun, moon, and stars. To date, I do not believe anything in world history fits this extreme description. Therefore, I conclude that the events described in Revelation will happen in the future.

Before we get into the verse-by-verse commentary, it may be helpful to have a general summary of the events of Revelation. I like to over-simplify it this way:

- Following worldwide revival, the Church will be raptured from the Earth.

- God will release a series of conditions on the Earth with the purpose of delivering the Earth from Satan and its demonic inhabitants.

- A host of people will align themselves with the Beast and the False Prophet, and they will worship an image erected by the false prophet in direct objection to and rebellion against Jesus Christ.

- Many more people will turn to Christ during this time, and Satan's attempt to rule and govern this planet will prove to be less effective than most Bible teachers have assumed.

- Jesus will return, with the saints in tow, to finally defeat His enemies and establish His Kingdom on Earth.

As I've stated in previous chapters, I believe the events described in Revelation will happen *after* a massive harvest of believers is taken from the Earth, otherwise known as the Rapture.

I also believe (with all my heart) that prior to the Rapture the Church will rise to a role of global supremacy in the most positive sense. Billions will rush into the Kingdom in a revival of the authentic gospel spurred on by the very power and manifest presence of God. The next era of Christianity will be a glory era, a time when the Church will host the presence of God as His glory literally covers the Earth. With these things in mind, I have defined my eschatology with the assumptions that:

- The last days (which began at Jesus's birth) could continue for many more years, decades, or even centuries. As the Bible says, *"Long ago God spoke many times and in many ways to our ancestors through the prophets. And now **in these final days** he has spoken to us through his Son"* (Heb. 1:1–2).

- The events described in Revelation are future even though similar events took place in history on a much smaller scale.

- All believers in the Lord Jesus Christ will be caught up from the Earth before the events of Revelation unfold.

- The Church is currently on the rise, and the end-time harvest will be so massive that the majority of Earth's population will come to know, love, and worship Jesus Christ.

- Better days are in our future. Of course, difficulties will exist along the way (that has always been the case), but for the most part the Earth has many good and hopeful years ahead as the Kingdom of Jesus Christ influences and saturates the kingdoms of this world.

- The epicenter of global revival could once again be Israel.

- The Church will lead the world into an era of prosperity, peace, and advancement. God will grant us solutions and technology advancements in all spheres of science, agriculture, and information.

- After a massive display of His power to protect Israel, God will pour out His Spirit and His glory all over the world simultaneously, and the irresistible goodness of God will draw most people groups to Himself.

AN INCONVENIENT TRUTH

One of the hardest books of the Bible to grasp is the book of Revelation—not because we can't understand what it is saying but because it is hard to reconcile these events with the goodness of God and the love of Jesus Christ for even the vilest of sinners. Some have rejected the contents of Revelation and even the idea of Hell for this very reason. Yet I believe the Bible clearly prophesies the events of the Great Tribulation as well as an eternal place of suffering for those who have blatantly rejected the free gift of salvation made possible by Jesus's death and resurrection.

God Himself is not pleased to carry out the acts of Revelation. We see this in the text below, where the angels who are pouring out the bowl judgments for God are encouraging Him that He is doing the right thing. One angel chimes in, and then another angel speaks in agreement.

Then the third angel poured out his bowl on the rivers and springs of water, and they became blood. And I heard the angel of the waters saying: "You are righteous, O Lord, the One who is and

*who was and who is to be, because You have judged these things.
For they have shed the blood of saints and prophets, and You have
given them blood to drink. For it is their just due." And I heard
another from the altar saying, "Even so, Lord God Almighty, true
and righteous are Your judgments"* (Revelation 16:4–7).

God does not want any to perish—not even those who obstinately
rejected the global outpouring of God's presence—including signs,
wonders, and miracles—that will precede the Great Tribulation.
Thus, even during the cataclysms of the end-times events, many will
finally turn their hearts to Jesus Christ, be saved and be raptured right
out of the Tribulation. God will go to every extent to save as many as
possible, but He cannot force people to accept His offer. When the
Final Judgment comes, despite God's love, some people may remain
in opposition to His lordship, choosing instead to cast in their lot
with Satan. They will not be helpless victims of God's judgment but
willfully defiant people who have chosen their fate.

The word *revelation* comes from the Greek word *apokalypsis,*
meaning "to lay bare, unveil, or disclose."1 In other words,
Revelation is an unveiling of the person of Jesus Christ and a full
disclosure of His intentions. I have read, studied, and taught the book
of Revelation many times with a constant insistence that God is
always good. I believe I have discovered the goodness of this book
and the acts of love intended in these events. I hope we can all agree
that, at some point, this world needs to be literally purged of Satan
and the demons so that we can get on with eternity under the direct
governance of Jesus Christ in the flesh, face-to-face in our glorified
bodies. For this reason, I conclude that the events of Revelation are
unfortunate but inevitable. This is the way forward, the only way to
forever purge evil and enter into eternal bliss with God.

My goal is to be as brief as possible while, at the same time, giving as broad a view of these future events as possible. I also want to prove that God remains fully in His goodness and grace throughout the entire time, not willing that any should perish. At the end, there will be no innocent bystanders, yet by the goodness of God, many will be saved in the process.

With these foundations established, let's jump in to the specifics of the book of Revelation, beginning in Chapter 6. As much as possible, I will address events in their sequential order while tying them into the framework of the entire book. Because much of what we read in Revelation is also prophesied throughout the Old Testament, I have also done my best to accurately place the Old Testament prophecies in their proper context and application in Revelation. I suggest having your Bible handy so that you may easily follow along.

6. The Beginning of the End For Satan

REVELATION 4–8

In Revelation 4, Heaven is opened, and the apostle John is immediately "in the Spirit," gazing upon the throne of God. John witnesses a ceremony in which the scroll that could be the title deed to Earth is handed to Jesus Christ. Based on Heaven's response, we can see that in all the universe only one person qualifies to loosen the seals and peel open this document—Jesus. He is the only one.

Imagine yourself in a courtroom filled with court officials and witnesses who are all there to confirm what is about to take place. The reason for the meeting is for you to receive your inheritance. There is a rolled-up document that has been sealed with a blob of putty and impressed by a certain ring. The ring is one of a kind, and it is the very ring you are wearing. Attached to the seal is a note that says, "Whoever wears the ring that bears this seal may open this document." Everyone in the room looks around until eventually all eyes are fixed on you, the one who has the ring. Everyone is anxious for you to open the document because your inheritance includes the fate of their futures, too. They want you to claim your prize.

This is, in essence, what happens in Revelation 4 and 5. The difference is that the only one who can open this scroll is the one who has been slain for the sins of the world, Jesus Christ.

You are worthy to take the scroll, and to open its seals [release judgment]; *for You were slain, and have redeemed us to God by Your blood out of every tribe and tongue and people and nation, and have made us kings and priests to our God; and we shall reign on the earth* (Revelation 5:9–10).

As Jesus opens each of the seven seals that are on this scroll, a series of conditions or (more accurately) contingencies are released upon the Earth. This is the setting as we embark on an amazing journey through the book of Revelation.

REVELATION 6

THE FIRST SIX SEALS

In Revelation 6, the first series of conditions on the Earth are released by unpeeling the first six seals from the scroll. The first four seals are commonly called the four horsemen of the apocalypse. The first horsemen—a rider on a white horse carrying a bow, with a crown on his head—is the most ambiguous. He rides out *"conquering and to conquer"* (Rev. 6:2). Some say this is the antichrist; others say it is Jesus. Needless to say, this horseman has caused some confusion. My theory is that the rider on the white horse represents the ongoing victorious work of the Kingdom of Jesus Christ that is still gaining victories even in the midst of the Great Tribulation. Souls are still being won, sicknesses are still being healed, and demoniacs are still being delivered. There is a moment on the timeline when the Beast does *"make war with the saints and to overcome them"* (Rev 13:7), but this is a temporal season for the purpose of kindling God's wrath against the Beast. Until that point, even in the midst of the Great Tribulation, the Kingdom of Jesus Christ continues in conquering mode, just as Isaiah 9:7 prophesied: *"Of the increase of His government and peace there will be no end."*

The other riders carry with them campaigns of war, famine, hyperinflation, and disease, but the backdrop is a precondition of ongoing Kingdom conquest (see Rev. 6:3–9). As I said before, God is *"not willing that any should perish but that all would come to repentance"* (2 Pet. 3:9). Even the people in the Tribulation who had previously rejected Him will be exposed to an authentic representation of the gospel during the entire Tribulation scenario.

Next comes the fifth seal, which could be martyrs who are killed in the first wave of Christian persecution (see Rev. 6:9–11). I imagine it going something like this: After the Rapture, hundreds of thousands of people will make a decision for Jesus Christ. Churches will be packed with people who are in a state of shock in the wake of a few billion people vanishing from the Earth. Prior to the Rapture, the Church will have won the sentiments of even the unbelievers due to our outspoken love and generosity. When we all disappear, they will immediately know what happened as they text and Tweet each other things like "The Bible is true after all," and "I think it was what they called the Rapture." In a matter of days, massive numbers of people will influx into the Kingdom, and simultaneously, the demonic spirits of the Beast and the False Prophet will entice Earth's remaining unredeemed population into a massive persecution campaign to squelch the voice of the rapidly spreading new Church. As a result, these martyrs cry out for God's justice against the Beast and the False Prophet. For the present, they are told to wait, but their request will come up again soon—in Revelation 8.

In the sixth seal, Heaven responds to the persecution with a massive earthquake (see Rev. 6:10–17). Just like on the day when

115

Christ was crucified, the sun will become dark and the moon will become like blood. This could result from the massive amount of dust and ash residue that will fill the sky during the great earthquake. Where I live, in Redding, California, we occasionally have intense fire seasons when multiple forest fires burn at one time within a few miles of each other. At these times, I have seen the sun and moon turn blood red because of the ash in the sky.

John also mentions stars falling to the Earth, which is somewhat mystifying since an actual star falling to the Earth would completely destroy the planet. However, the word used in the Greek is *aster,* which means a literal star. I wonder whether debris from the stars, which has made its way into the Earth's atmosphere, might be the actual fulfillment of this verse. In fact, I have experienced an event like this, too, while driving through Wells, Nevada, on a summer night in 1999. A busload of teenagers and I were on our way home from a mission trip. Around midnight, the entire sky began to turn blood red as streamers fell across the horizon, tinting the nighttime glow totally red. We pulled the bus over and got out, oohing and aahing as the red streamers entered the atmosphere. I read in the newspaper a few days later that it was debris from the sun falling to the Earth. Since the sun is a star, that event in Nevada would qualify as a star falling to the Earth and account for the blood red Sun and Moon that John saw.

Interestingly, in verses 15–17, the world leaders know full well that these events are *"from the wrath of the Lamb."* The prophet Isaiah anticipated what appears to be the same scenario when he prophesied: *"Crawl into caves in the rocks. Hide in the dust from the terror of the Lord and the glory of his majesty"* (Isa. 2:10). The phrases the wrath of the Lamb and the terror of the Lord are not great ones to use when evangelizing, and it is not an attitude that Heaven displays toward humanity any time soon. Rather, it is reserved for a specific time period, of which Revelation 6 is the kick off.

REVELATION 7:1–8

ALL THE YOUNG DUDES

The next chapter begins with an amazing event about 144,000 Jews. Later, in Revelation 14, these 144,000 Jews also get a personal visitation from Jesus in the midst of the Tribulation, but here they are sealed, which I take as a mark from the Lord that brands them as untouchable by those who are attempting to destroy the people of God. In Revelation 14, these 144,000 are described as those who are *"not defiled with women, for they are virgins"* (Rev. 14:4) and as those who *"have told no lies"* and *"are without blame"* (Rev. 14:5 NLT). To help establish the identity of these 144,000, I want to recall the time when Jesus sat a child on His lap and taught about the Kingdom:

> *At the same time came the disciples unto Jesus, saying, Who is the greatest in the kingdom of heaven? And Jesus called a little child unto him, and set him in the midst of them, And said, Verily I say unto you, Except ye be converted, and become as little children, ye shall not enter into the kingdom of heaven. Whosoever therefore shall humble himself as this little child, the same is greatest in the kingdom of heaven. And whoso shall receive one such little child in my name receives me. But whoso shall offend one of these little ones which believe in me, it were better for him that a millstone were hanged about his neck, and that he were drowned in the depth of the sea (Matthew 18:1–6 KJV).*

My theory is that the 144,000 virgins who are without blame are male children—possibly all first born males. In fact, I think this relates back to the first Passover during the Exodus. In the book of Numbers, it says:

> *The Lord spoke to Moses saying: "Now behold I have taken the Levites from among the children of Israel instead of every firstborn who opens the womb among the children of Israel. Therefore the Levites shall be Mine,* **because all the firstborn are mine, on that day I struck all the firstborn in the land of Egypt, I sanctified to Myself all the firstborn in Israel"** (Numbers 3:11–13).

Thus, these 144,000 male children are like the Levites who were sanctified to the Lord. This is why Revelation 14:4 calls them the *"firstfruits to God and to the Lamb."*

An interesting verse from Isaiah also speaks about the time of the Tribulation and possibly gives credence to my idea about the role of the 144,000: *"I will give children to be their princes and babes shall rule over them"* (Isa. 3:4). During the time of the Tribulation, Israel and Jerusalem will no doubt become devoid of national leadership and preservation. Many will have to flee the city and even the country (following Jesus's instructions in Matthew 24:15– 22), leaving Jerusalem desolate and unprotected. Though this city is in the direct crosshairs of the Beast's campaign, some will have to remain for various reasons. The elderly who live alone, orphans, mentally ill. The poor, lame and the destitute. There will be all kinds of helpless people who will not be able to flee. It is this small remnant that, I believe, might be governed and even protected by the 144,000 boys who are supernaturally sustained through it all.

The prophecy in Isaiah 3 supports this. No one will want to be the leader of the nation. All will be intimidated by the Beast nations that are taking over their land. None of the people will want to be next to be drug through the streets or to have their houses invaded by angry, hungry mobs.

In those days a man will say to his brother, "Since you have a coat, you be our leader! Take charge of this heap of ruins!" But he will reply, "No! I can't help. I don't have any extra food or clothes. Don't put me in charge!" (Isaiah 3:6–7 NLT).

Yet amazingly, even in the midst of all this, the godly will be preserved. Isaiah continued with these words of encouragement: *"Tell the godly that all will be well for them. They will enjoy the rich reward they have earned"* (Isa. 3:10). The preserving power of God is amazing. I can't help but be encouraged. The people of God are able to live according to Heaven's economy and favor, even when the governments of the Earth are making terrible decisions. This isn't just true for the Tribulation, but for all time. I've seen it fleshed out in my own life.

After these 144,000 boys, who may be the rulers of the Jewish remnant, are sealed by God, they make their way to Jerusalem, to theTemple Mount, during the events of the Tribulation. There they stay on Mount Zion, where they wait for Jesus. Help is on the way. They have been sealed by the Lord, and they can't be touched or harmed in any way. Finally, as the Great Tribulation unfolds, Jesus joins them: *"Then I saw the Lamb standing on Mount Zion, and with him were the 144,000 who had his name and his Father's name written on their foreheads"* (Rev. 14:1 NLT). When at last they meet Jesus, Heaven responds with great joy as they sing a brand new song written especially for the event.

REVELATION 7:9–17

THE GRATEFUL DEAD

The remainder of Revelation 7 gives us a vision of Heaven's throne room, where a multitude cries out in worship of God. It is clear these saints died during the Great Tribulation; in other words, they were not among the raptured but were those who converted afterward. As we've already mentioned, after the Rapture, many new believers will accept Jesus, but because the Church no longer has overwhelming influence over the nations, Satan, the Great Dragon, wastes no time throwing the world into famine, casting many from their homes and villages.

In verse 16, the angel tells John that now *"they will never be hungry or thirsty; they will never be scorched by the heat of the sun."* From this, I assume these people died from starvation and exposure. I can only imagine what would happen in extremely hot and arid parts of the world if millions of people were displaced and forced into the desert without food or water. Thankfully, they are met with open arms in Heaven and a promise of no more thirst, starvation, or heat exhaustion.

REVELATION 8:1–5

THE SILENCE IS DEAFENING

Revelation 8 begins with a fascinating event: silence in Heaven for half an hour, which is the seventh seal. I can hardly imagine complete silence for half an hour here on Earth, let alone in *Heaven,* where praise is continually offered before the throne. Obviously, the tone of the moment is incredibly serious. The first series of judgments—the six seals—have already been released. Now, the situation on Earth is about to get worse. We are venturing into deep waters that most folks (including me) do not like to read regarding the future of a remnant of humanity and this Earth. However, we must remember that the Church has been removed after the multi-billion soul harvest, and (as we saw in the last section) a multitude of others who got saved after the Rapture are now in Heaven worshipping God. The number of Satan's victims is getting smaller and smaller.

Overall, the situation has become so awful that God has great incentive to expedite the timeline. It's also important to keep in mind that all of the people who remain on the Earth have rejected Jesus Christ as Lord or are the offspring of and are still under the authority of those who did. Many are getting saved as they realize that the campaign of the powers-that-be are not in their best interest, as they had supposed, yet I believe many people will still refuse Christ as Lord, very possibly out of fear of retribution.

Here is a modern example of this sort of scenario. A few years ago, Israel gave a small strip of land away to the Palestinian people. Almost overnight, the infamous terrorist organization, Hamas, moved in among the people and starting firing rockets over the border into Israel. Eventually Israel was forced to respond, and in the melee, Palestinian civilians are killed. One could wonder why the Palestinian people don't speak out against Hamas. After all, if Hamas left, their homes and businesses would no longer be bombed and destroyed. The answer is simple: fear. It's hard for me to imagine that the Palestinian people are actually supportive of these terrorists. But they know that if they speak up, they stand a chance of being killed and drug through the street as an example. That very thing has already happened there. Similarly, in the midst of the Great Tribulation, accepting Christ will come with a strong possibility of martyrdom.

Having said that, I also believe many people groups around the world may be relatively safe from the campaign of the Beast and the False Prophet because of proximity. Don't get me wrong here. The catastrophic events taking place in the *kosmos* is enough tribulation in and of itself. But I do think many survivors of the Tribulation will walk right into the Millennial Kingdom. Even though they haven't been technically born again, they didn't take the mark of the Beast, either. As a result, Jesus will evangelize them personally (something I will discuss in detail later).

My point is this: Even in the midst of the Tribulation, God is still good, and His desire toward humanity is still that all would be saved. A significant portion of those who remain on the Earth at the beginning of the second series of judgments are defiantly refusing God's grace toward them and are throwing their lot in with the Beast nations. With this backdrop, let's keep reading.

THE SAINTS WEIGH IN

After the seventh seal silence in Heaven, seven angels are given seven trumpets, which will release judgments on the Earth. The seventh seal is divided into seven parts. Because of the severity of this seal, the Lord sees fit to unleash it incrementally. Each portion is released by a blast from a trumpet. The following events, which escalate the mayhem on Earth, are in response to *"the prayers of God's holy people"* (Rev. 8:3 NLT). This refers back to the fifth seal, where those martyred during the Great Tribulation cry out for justice:

> *I saw under the altar the soul of all who had been martyred for the word of God and for being faithful in their testimony. They shouted to the Lord and said, "O Sovereign Lord, holy and true, how long before you judge the people who belong to this world and avenge our blood for what they have done to us?"* (Revelation 6:9–10 NLT).

In response, they are told to: *Rest a little longer until the full number of their brothers and sisters—their fellow servants who were to be martyred—had joined them* (Revelation 6:11 NLT).

I suggest that the seventh seal events are the tipping of the scale. Up to this point, the people of God have been praying for mercy on the Earth. They are fueled by supernatural love and desire to see as many people come into the Kingdom as possible. But now even the grace-filled, mercy-loving Christians on the Earth have said, "Enough is enough!" They just can't take any more. They can't handle seeing any more infants die, seeing any more people displaced and starved to death, seeing the rise of evil in unprecedented measure. In Revelation 6, the first words of the martyrs under the altars are words of vengeance. I doubt this is a normal response from martyrs as they enter Heaven. Instead, this unusual cry for revenge is birthed by the extreme evil of God's enemies on Earth.

Finally, the feeling is unanimous. The saints on the Earth and the martyrs in Heaven agree, and the Lord must comply. From this sequence, I conclude that the cataclysmic events from here on out are directly requested by the Church—both the martyred Church and those who remain on Earth. The Lord has purposely made Himself vulnerable to the Church and relies heavily on our prayers and activities to thrust His will forward. For the first time in eternity, He hears a unanimous call for vengeance.

As I mentioned previously, this belief that the Lord responds directly to the prayers of His people is one of the reasons I believe the Church has to be raptured before the final days. The end-times Church will walk in the fullness of our identity. Thus, our presence on the Earth could hinder the final stages of God's plan to get rid of Satan and his demonic army. Now that the raptured Church is with

Jesus, a new Church has sprung up on the Earth in the midst of the Tribulation. This Church understands fully the time they are living in and recognizes their role and the power of prayer in unleashing God's judgments against the forces of evil. The tide has turned, and even the saints are saying, *"Avenge our blood for what they have done to us"* (Rev. 6:10 NLT).

As we will see later, during the fourth trumpet, an eagle cries loudly, *"Terror, terror, terror to all who belong to this world..."* (Rev. 8:13 NLT). I believe the emphasis is *this world*. In other words, the world is not the same without the direct influence of the victorious and mature Church. The salt of the Earth is gone by design so that the Lord can allow Satan's agenda to play out. This world of the Great Tribulation is destined to crumble. Many of the people of *this world* are dead set against Jesus. But as we will see in the coming chapters, many more will get saved and be harvested in the midst of all the chaos.

REVELATION 8:6–13

ANGELS BLOW YOUR HORN

Thus, because of the prayers of the saints, the angels take their places and prepare to blow their trumpets, which will each release a judgment upon the Earth. Because I am not a scientist or a meteorologist, I don't feel particularly adequate to describe how these events will happen. For now, I will stick to the obvious. The first four trumpets are global and cataclysmic. Here's my incredibly brilliant interpretation: Large things from outer space will hit the Earth and ruin the atmosphere and the ecosystem. As a very observant eagle sums it up, *"Terror, terror, terror to all who belong to this world because of what will happen when the last three angels blow their trumpets"* (Rev. 8:13 NLT).

In just a few pages, I have summarized the initial events of the Great Tribulation. Moving into Revelation 9 and the final three trumpet judgments, an important shift happens—from cataclysmic eco-disasters to demonic manifestations. In the face of this rapid escalation of such bizarre events, many theologians have reduced the previous and following events to hyperbole. However, I do not believe (as some have suggested) that John was struggling for words to explain what he saw. Rather, we are the ones who are grappling to understand and believe the potential of these claims. God does not have a communication problem; we have a belief problem. With that in mind, in the next chapter we continue our journey into the bizarre and temporal world of the Great Tribulation.

7. We Have Visitors

REVELATION 9–12

In the following texts, I am committed to not over-thinking the content in order to reconcile what I have read. In many schools of eschatological thought, the allegories based on these passages run wild. I, however, will do my best to stay grounded and simple. One thing I have learned over the past few years of my own ministry of healing the sick is that understanding the things of God is less important than believing them and acting on them.

As we read, we must remember that John was seeing into the spiritual realm. He was in Heaven looking down toward Earth, and he was able to see what was going on in the invisible realms in-between. Perhaps the reason most of this seems so fantastic to us is the fact that we normally do not see in the spirit. However, at the end, I believe these demonic forces may become visible and manifest to those on Earth during that particular time.

The story of Elisha's servant illustrates this well:

When the servant of the man of God got up early the next morning and went outside, there were troops, horses, and chariots everywhere. "Oh, sir, what will we do now?" the young man cried to Elisha. "Don't be afraid!" Elisha told him. "For there are more on our side than on theirs!" Then Elisha prayed, "O LORD, open his eyes and let him see!" The LORD opened the young man's eyes, and when he looked up, he saw that the hillside around Elisha was filled with horses and chariots of fire (2 Kings 6:15–17 NLT).

The young man who accompanied Elijah was given a view into the spiritual realm, and suddenly he saw the invisible army of God. Likewise, the apostle John was seeing the armies of hell. No allegories are needed here.

REVELATION 9:1–12

THE REAL HELLS ANGELS

When the fifth trumpet is blown, Hell is opened up, and the locusts (demons) are loosed. In a brazen flurry, they attack any who are not sealed by the Lord. One popular interpretation of this passage says the stinging locusts are actually armies and modern military hardware, for example helicopters, missiles, and tanks. I personally think they are literal demonic manifestations. The fact that *"their king is the angel of the bottomless pit"* and his name means "destroyer" adds credence to the idea that these locusts are actually demons (see Rev. 9:10). However, if I wanted to use symbolism, I could make a better case that the critters in verses 7–12 are a motorcycle gang. After all, they have gold crowns (helmets), human faces, women's hair, teeth like a lion, and armor made of iron, and to top it all off, their wings roar like an army of chariots rushing into battle. You can almost hear the *vroom, vroom, vroooooooom*. I only add this poke at the tendency toward theological symbolism and the overuse of it to make a point. We can easily paint all kinds of pictures with such unusual texts, yet often our allegories end up being more dramatic than the text itself.

Joel 1:6 describes a similar locust army, only Joel's prophecy is about an event that actually flows right into the Lord's return, starting at chapter 2. The locusts in Joel's account strip the fig trees bare and ruin the crops (see Joel 1:7), which directly violates the parameters the locusts are given in Revelation 9:4. Considering this, I believe, it is probably a different locust attack. Alternatively, perhaps the locusts in Revelation 9:4 disobeyed the command not to harm the vegetation. Whether these are the same event or not, we can be certain that these demon locusts will be fearsome creatures. Imagining them reminds me of these words of Jesus:

> *Then the seventy returned with joy, saying, "Lord, even the demons are subject to us in Your name." And He said to them, "I saw Satan fall like lightning from heaven. Behold, **I give you the authority to trample on serpents and scorpions, and over all the power of the enemy, and nothing shall by any means hurt you.** Nevertheless do not rejoice in this, that the spirits are subject to you, but rather rejoice because your names are written in heaven"* (Luke 10:17–20).

I'm sure these words will be taken very literally by those who will be sealed for protection from this demonic army, as well as those who get born again during these traumatic events.

These sorts of demonic manifestations may seem unbelievable to some, but I believe they are already happening on a much smaller scale. During the Great Tribulation, what is now for the most part hidden will be seen by everyone. I have talked personally with people who minister at the Pine Ridge Indian reservation in South Dakota, and multiple witnesses told me that demons have been seen roaming the city in broad day light. One pastor from the reservation told me that they have seen demons manifest in the form of large serpents slithering through town, spanning across buildings.

My son and I once delivered a woman from demons in Costa Rica. Her husband had asked us to come. According to her husband and her son, they heard some weird noises coming from the upstairs balcony. The son was in his room and the husband downstairs. When they came to see what was going on, they saw the mother crawling on the floor and manifesting like a bug while a visible demon danced on top of her. After about five hours of ministry, she was beautifully delivered, and two days later we saw her in church with three of her family members at her side. She was standing with both hands in the air worshipping God.

Thirty-five years ago, when I was eighteen years old, I had an encounter with a visible demon. I wasn't following Jesus at the time. The demon appeared in my room and stood over me, speaking in what I will call satanic tongues. I was able to interpret his speech, and I understood that he was warning me to avoid the Bible because it wasn't true. When I rebuked him in the name of Jesus, he fled, sucking all the oxygen from the room as he left. Suddenly, my room was freezing cold.

These are just a few examples. Many, many people have encountered visible demonic spirits. In some parts of the world, it is extremely common. The reason I share these demon stories is to stir our minds to the reality that these stinging locusts from the bottomless pit are not that farfetched when compared to many manifestations of the demonic that people have witnessed *prior* to the end-time wrath of the Lamb. For this reason, I believe the events of the fifth trumpet are not allegorical but will happen exactly the way John wrote it, stinging locusts and all.

REVELATION 9:13–21

TWO HUNDRED MILLION HORSEMEN

I apply the same principal to the sixth trumpet—two hundred million horsemen release plagues on the Earth, killing one third of the population by breathing out fire, smoke, and brimstone.

Some interpret this passage as a military invasion from China, saying that China is the only nation that could amass a two hundred million person army. Others claim John was trying to describe modern artillery without the language for it. However, I find no reason to assume China is the culprit here. Certainly that kind of theology doesn't help missionary efforts there. (For the record, the People's Liberation Army of China currently has only about three million personnel.)

Yet I believe the movie trilogy, *The Lord of the Rings*, which has landscapes filled with demon-like orcs, gives our imaginations a better context for envisioning how these events might play out. Based on my belief that the Rapture will significantly decrease the world population, I doubt any country during the Tribulation will be capable of amassing such a large army. Rather, I believe the entire military force of Revelation 9 is a demonic army.

In the first part of chapter 9, the bottomless pit was opened, and the demon locusts came forth to torment (but not kill) people for five months. It makes sense to me that, following those months, another demonic force would be released that would kill one third of the population. Envisioning the army as demonic also makes it easier to understand how they can breathe fire, smoke, and brimstone from their mouths. Satan, the Dragon, has but three goals: destroy humans, destroy the Earth, and destroy Jesus. With this in mind, it should be no surprise that demons would enact destruction as locusts and as a fire-breathing army. As we will see in Revelation 11:5, God has His fire-breathers, too.

It is important to notice here that, even in the mist of such terror, the Lord will still look for a harvest. Unfortunately, *"the people who did not die in these plagues still refused to repent of their evil deeds and turn to God"* (Rev. 9:20). I am positive the Lord's heart will respond with sadness. When we read the statement, we must think in terms of sorrow and regret. Many a preacher has blurted out that line with an attitude that I don't believe represents the heart of a loving Father. These unrepentant people are His own children, made in His own image. He takes no delight in their destruction.

REVELATION 10

ENOUGH IS ENOUGH

Revelation 10 tells of a mighty angel with a little book in his hand, which John is told to eat. When he does, it tastes sweet in his mouth but becomes bitter in his stomach. Based on the description of this angel, he seems to be none other than Jesus Christ. He is *"clothed with a cloud,"* and He has a *"rainbow on His head,"* a *"face like the sun,"* and *"feet like pillars of fire."* This description is very similar to how John describes Jesus in Revelation 1 (see Rev. 1:15–16; 14:1). Also, the word used here for *angel* is, in the Greek, *aggelos,* which simply means "a messenger sent from God."1 Jesus is personally delivering the little book to John. The result is a bittersweet experience—bitter because of what has to happen in the final stages of the Tribulation, but sweet because of the end result. Jesus will be King on this Earth.

The main point here is at the end of verse 6: *"There will be no more delay"* (NLT). The suffering on the Earth will be beyond comprehension, and we know the Lord takes no pleasure in the death of the wicked. He certainly finds no enjoyment in the steady stream of martyrs. Thus, the time has come to remove even more restraints and let Satan escalate his inevitable tantrum for the purpose of once and for all routing the devil and getting on with the Kingdom.

In verse 7 we read: *"When the seventh angel blows his trumpet, Gods mysterious plan will be fulfilled. It will happen just as he announced it to his servants the prophets"* (NLT). Then John eats the book, receiving the rest of the Revelation prophecy, and is told, *"You must prophecy again about many peoples, nations, languages and kings"* (Rev. 10:11 NLT). This is the framework and purpose for the rest of the judgments, beginning with the seventh trumpet in Revelation 11.

REVELATION 11

DOS HOMBRES CON FUEGO

However, before the seventh trumpet blasts, two fascinating characters appear on the scene—the two witnesses. At this point, we can assume we are midway into the tribulation scenario. Now the focus turns toward the temple. This is because, in my opinion, when Jesus comes back, He will build a new temple right on the Temple Mount. While He was on Earth, He said, *"Destroy this temple, and in three days I will raise it up"* (John 2:9). He was speaking of His bodily resurrection, but I believe He also may have been prophesying about this coming temple.

So at the beginning of Revelation 11, John is told to measure the temple but not the outer court because it has been given over to the gentiles (some Bibles translate this as "nations"). Given this, many think the outer court is the place where the Dome of the Rock shrine currently stands. It's possible, though no one can say for sure. Regardless, the point is that Jesus plans to have a temple, and to

133

emphasize this, He sends two ambassadors from Heaven—the two witnesses—to declare His plans.

These two witnesses are described as *"the two olive trees and the two lampstands standing before the God of the earth"* (Rev. 11:4). To fully understand their role and identity, you should read Zechariah 4, where we also see a lampstand and two olive trees that are symbols of prophets and ambassadors of the coming temple. Zechariah 4:14 calls them *"the two anointed ones, who stand beside the Lord of the whole earth."* These guys are mysterious for sure, but I'm certain they will prophecy to the world that Jesus is coming back and that a new temple will be rebuilt right there on the Temple Mount. Whether or not the rebuilt temple exists prior to Jesus's return, I believe Jesus will at some point rebuild His own perfect model, and here He sends two *fire- breathing* witnesses from Heaven to declare it (see Rev. 11:5).

Some believe the two witnesses are Moses and Elijah because they were seen with Jesus on the mount of transfiguration and because of the power and authority they have (see Rev. 11:6). We don't know that for sure, and it really doesn't matter who they are. The power Moses and Elijah walked in came from God, and the same will be true of the two witnesses. God can use anybody He wants. Once the witnesses have finished prophesying (1260 days), they will be killed by Apollyon (the lord of the pit from Revelation 9:11). However, they are then resurrected and caught up into Heaven.

The question is: What is the point or, better yet, the importance of the two witnesses? We see a clue in the events of the seventh trumpet, which happens immediately after these two witnesses are caught up into Heaven. *"Then the seventh angel sounded: And there were loud voices shouting in heaven: "the world has now become the*

Kingdom of our Lord and of His Christ, and he will reign forever" (Rev. 11:15).

In the real estate business, what the two witnesses did is called the completion of a contingency. They came as representatives of the Kingdom of Heaven and made a public proclamation that this land is under new ownership and on such and such a day there will be a new building right here on this location. It's as if the current structures are being condemned and plans for a new state-of-the-art facility are being publicized. The response of the twenty-four elders confirms this. I call them Heaven's Board of Directors. Here's what they say in verse 17, *"...You have assumed your great power and have begun to reign"* (NLT). In essence, chapter 11 is giving us details about the actual transaction of Christ's reclamation of the Earth. Now all He has to do is finish evicting the tenants-from-hell. It's like a celebratory escrow closing.

Based on what follows in Revelation 12, I believe—after the elders celebrate the return of the two witnesses to Heaven, knowing the final contingency has been fulfilled and the public announcement of a new temple and coming King has been made—they toss the devil out of Heaven. Until that point in time, he will be accusing the brethren night and day before the throne of God (see Rev. 12:10).

REVELATION 12

SATAN GETS THE BOOT

This is the framework for Revelation 12, which gives us a broad review, or timeline, to fill in some blanks and set the stage for the coming events. The scene on Earth is about to heat up because Satan has been forced down to the Earth, where he will be dealt with once and for all. No longer is he allowed access before God's throne. I like to think of chapter 12 as Heaven's courtroom review of the main events of Satan's career. At the end, without much debate, they say, "You are out of here! Bye, bye!"

THE HISTORY OF A NATION IN A NUTSHELL

Because this chapter is rife with very significant symbolism, it needs more detailed coverage than some of the others. I will do my best to be brief, so hang on for a whirlwind of a ride!

The first verses condense the nation of Israel (see Gen. 37:5–11) into on single representative woman, the virgin Mary, who literally becomes pregnant and gives birth (see Rev. 12:1–2). As she gives birth, a multi-headed dragon appears and tries to devour her child as he is born (see Rev. 12:3–4). (This same dragon, which has seven heads with seven crowns, as well as ten horns, makes another appearance in Revelation 17). We could speculate from now until Christ returns about who the seven heads wearing the seven crowns are. Some say Roman Caesars. Others argue for rulers of a revived Roman empire. Still others suggest various Islamic rulers or Arabic Sheikdoms. Each position has some good arguments and some weaknesses. I say the jury is still out.

What we do know is who the dragon is—the devil (see Rev. 12:9). Therefore, we can safely conclude that, in the context of our story, a satanically-influenced leader *"stood in front of the woman as she was about to give birth, ready to devour her baby as soon as it was born"* (Rev. 12:4 NLT). This line seems to clearly speak of King Herod's attempt to kill the Christ child (see Matt. 2).

Despite the dragon's efforts, Jesus is born and eventually ascends to Heaven to sit beside God (see Rev. 12:5). Then the woman (Israel) flees to the wilderness to hide for three and a half years. I believe this will happen following the Abomination of Desolation. Seeing it, the Jews will flee to the wilderness as Jesus warned them. There they will be fed by God. Many people believe this place of refuge is the ancient rock city, Petra, in Jordan. Built as a desert oasis by the ancient Nabataeans, the city was engineered in such a way as to capture all the rain water into pools during the rainy season. This enabled the Nabataeans to live there year round. I believe placing the Jew's wilderness experience in Petra may explain what happens later (in verses 15–16).

However, before we get to that, we read of the war that breaks out in Heaven as Satan and his demons are permanently exiled from Heaven. At this point, Heaven throws a party but also cautions the Earth: *"Woe to the inhabitants of the earth and the sea! For the devil has come down to you, having great wrath, because he knows that he has a short time"* (Rev. 12:12). As expected, Satan's exile infuriates him and causes his persecution of the woman to increase. It says the dragon spews water from his mouth like a flood but that the Earth swallows the flood and saves the woman. If I am reading this correctly, it seems like Satan attempts to flood the Jews out of their hiding place (which would make a lot of sense if, in fact, it is Petra); however, the water is swallowed up by the Earth.

At this point, Psalm 31 offers us an interesting prophecy regarding a season of distress. In my opinion, in the final verses of this psalm, David prophesied of a future time when His people will be forced to seek refuge from a great oppression—perhaps even the Great Tribulation.

Oh how great is Your goodness which You have laid up for those who fear You. Which You have prepared for those who trust in You in the presence of the sons of men! You shall hide them in the secret place of Your presence from the plots of man; You shall keep them secretly in a pavilion from the strife of tongues. Blessed be the Lord, for He has shown me His marvelous kindness in a strong city. For I said in my haste I am cut off from before Your eyes; nevertheless You heard the voice of my supplications when I cried to You. Oh love the Lord, all you His saints! For the Lord preserves the faithful... (Psalm 31:19–22).

Years ago my church hosted a Jews for Jesus team and had an amazing weekend of ministry with them. One of the girls on the team told me that when Sadaam Hussein was shooting scud missiles into Israel, the rabbis in many of the bomb shelters read prophecy from the Psalms that they believed applied directly to the situation. It's not hard to imagine this being the case when Israel faces such a great challenge as the Beast and the False Prophet in the Tribulation.

Two words in David's psalm, in particular, cause me to believe this psalm applies to this event. First, the word *pavilion* (cukkah in Hebrew), meaning "a temporary shelter,"2 reminds me of the Jew's need to flee their homes and hide in a temporary location. Second, the phrase *strong city* speaks of their need for protection from the forces outside their shelter. If, in fact, they will seek refuge in the ancient city of Petra, they would be literally taken care of by God in a temporary shelter that does qualify architecturally as a strong city. Petra is carved right out of the cliffs and the rocks. The city of Petra was designed by the ancient Nabataeans to actually catch and retain rain water. Many of the travel guides about the city today caution tourists to be careful to get off the streets during heavy rain-storms in order to avoid drowning or being washed down the street. It is, no doubt, a strong city that one can drown in. Regardless of the actual location, we know that Satan's attempts to drown them are unsuccessful. Thus, he focuses his persecution on *"the rest of her offspring, who keep the commandments of God and have the testimony of Jesus Christ"* (Rev. 12:17).

All these events—the demonic hoards from the pit, the mighty angel with the little book, the two witnesses and their declaration of the coming temple and king, the expulsion of Satan and his persecution of the Jews and Christians—are building toward the culmination of world history. The dragon positions himself along the sea, preparing to call forth the Beast nations (see Rev. 12:18 NLT), and the Lamb readies His army of saints (see Rev. 14:1). But as you will see Satan has deceived himself most of all.

8. Satan Your Kingdom Must Come Down

REVELATION 13–15

Robert Plant and his Band of Joy performed an old blues song, written in 1931 by Blind Joe Taggart, called "Satan Your Kingdom Must Come Down." They did an amazing job with that song. Its storyline—the fall of Satan's empire—is what we are about to read. Most of the comments I hear about these chapters in Revelation focus almost entirely on the rise of Satan's kingdom. However, as we will soon see, it is only his *attempt* at setting up a kingdom. This entire book is about the dismantling of Satan's kingdom! Let me reemphasize this, the book of Revelation is not about the rise of the antichrist! It is about the final dismantling of Satan's kingdom, the expiration of his dominion, and his last ditch effort to unsuccessfully prop it up. The entire Tribulation scenario is only seven years long, and Satan's attempted global coup technically doesn't start until the midway point, which is hardly enough time to rule the entire planet, as some suppose. Rather, this is the story of Satan's failed attempt at world domination. Throughout the saga, Satan's kingdom is crashing faster than he can build it. The text tells us of Satan's attempted exploits, but it also tells us that Jesus continues to pull the rug out from under him and to harvest more souls for the Kingdom along the way.

To fully understand the series of events recorded in Revelation 13–15, we need to understand that each chapter provides simultaneous and overlapping scenarios. Some people isolate them as singular events due to the chapter breaks, which weren't part of the original text. Rather, I recommend a fast reading of these three chapters, as if it was the culmination of an action-packed novel's build-up. I find that the New Living Translation helps for a swift reading since the language is more like the way we talk today.

REVELATION 13

THE RISE OF THE BEASTS

Revelation 13 is one of the most famous chapters of the entire Bible. Even nonbelievers and Satanists study its contents. When our ministry owned a used bookstore in Jerome, Idaho, I use to peruse all the boxes of donations for commentaries and other books of personal interest. Once, I stumbled upon a mid-sixties commentary on Revelation by Louis Talbot. When I picked it up and held it by its spine it fell open to Revelation 13. That particular chapter had been referred to so many times that even today the book opens automatically to the section on Revelation 13.

Based on the sequence of Revelation, I believe, by this point, the grand scenario presented in the previous chapter will have already happened. After Satan fails to destroy the Jews who have fled to the wilderness, he turns his attention toward the rest of God's people— Jew and Christian alike. He stands on the seashore as if to summon the two Beasts—the first Beast rising *"out of the sea"* and the second Beast rising *"out of the earth"* (Rev. 13:1,11). These two Beasts are often combined into one figure, called the Beast, which symbolizes a conglomerate of nations that will join forces with Satan to wage war against God. The prophet Daniel gives us some identifying language about this Beast:

The fourth beast shall be a fourth kingdom on earth, which shall be different from all other kingdoms, and shall devour the whole earth, trample it and break it in pieces. The ten horns are ten kings who shall arise from this kingdom... (Daniel 7:23–24).

The union between Satan (the Dragon) and the Beast nations result in a full-blown attempt at a power-grab, through which they aim to control and manipulate humanity by all means necessary. This includes producing deceptive miracles and demanding that the people of the Earth give allegiance to them (take the mark of the Beast) in order to participate in the economy.

DEFINING THE MARK

Much speculation has circulated regarding what the mark of the Beast might be—most of it based in fear. So let me start of by saying what it isn't. It is not a computer chip under the skin. That idea is a joke; technology has come so far that the need to put a chip in a person for identification is laughable. Retina scans and finger print recognition are already old technologies. Rather, the mark of the Beast is the willful embracing of Satan's agenda. It is the decision to join with the Beast in an effort and belief that Jesus will not take back the Earth. It is the equivalent of putting on the uniform of Satan's army, waving the flag, and wearing a cap with His logo on it. When people accept the mark of the Beast, they become card-carrying union members of Satan's tribe. Whatever it will be and however it will look exactly is yet to be seen.

Six Six Six

Revelation 13 ends with this cryptic statement, which has also caused great fascination and speculation: *"Here is wisdom. Let him who has understanding calculate the number of the beast, for it is the number of a man: His number is 666"* (Rev 13:18). Some translations say 616. Many people have spent a great deal of energy trying to decipher who the Beast will be (or was) using Gematria, Hebrew numerology used to interpret Scripture by computing the numeric value of words.

When it comes to understanding 666, we need to expand our thinking beyond just names. Sure, the number could be the symbol of a name, but it could be a symbol for something else. For example, Walid Shoebat, a convert from Islam to Christianity, makes a fairly convincing case that the numbers 666 or 616 were actually a symbol John saw that represent Islamic Jihad. Even though the Muslim religion would not be established for another 515 years, Shoebat believes John wrote down a symbol he saw that looked similar to the Greek symbols for the number 666.1

One of the most well-known interpretations is the preterist view that Caesar Nero is the Beast based on the name Nero equaling 666— that is, if you spell his name Neron. This is a well-documented position with lots of research. However, Caesar Nero just doesn't fit the bill. As proven earlier in this book, he only partially fulfilled the prophecies about the Beast, thus making him an incomplete candidate. And the book of Revelation has too much language that clearly dovetails these events into the very last days, just prior to Christ's triumphant return. I am not sure anyone has figured the mystery of 666 out yet, but I'm certain it will be clear *by the time it's relevant*. Unfortunately, so much of the fascination with this number has grown from the fear Christians have of undergoing the Great

Tribulation and the persecution of the Beast. Let us remember, by that time, the Church will be in Heaven with Jesus. And the believers who are alive at that time will no doubt have clarity on this issue. We know this because, in Revelation 14:9– 10, an angel literally flies through the sky warning them not to take the mark. I assume they will know what the angel is referring to. The angel seems to think so.

THE THRONE OF SATAN

Many ascribe the number 666 to the "antichrist," though (as we've already discussed) no such figure exists in the Bible. It does talk about the Dragon, the Beast, the second Beast (who rises out of the first), the False Prophet, and finally the image of the Beast. In fact, it is actually the image of the Beast, which has been "given life," that calls for universal allegiance and acceptance of the mark (see Rev. 13:15). So when we get down to the nitty-gritty, the one commonly referred to as the "antichrist" is actually a statue that talks. And the statue is made in the image of the first Beast, who is actually a conglomeration of nations. In other words, this "antichrist" is not even a single person, but an image of a group of nations. It is certainly confusing, but I think I have a handle on it.

If you accurately and meticulously follow the Scripture trail, the "spirit of antichrist" (see 1 John 2:18,22; 4:3; 2 John 1:7) that has been alive and at work in the world since the apostle John's day and throughout human history has woven its way through various governments of the world, including the Roman Empire, and it is still at work today. In the end-times, it will eventually manifest in a statue or an idol that speaks. In other words, in the future a literal demon will bypass his typical method of speaking through a person and will begin to speak directly to the world using a graven image as its body. Now we understand why God has made it clear that His people are not to use idols in any form of our worship.

Along these lines, I believe the demonic spirit of antichrist ruled from the Pergamon Altar, located in Pergamos during the time of Jesus. In the seven letters to the seven churches, Jesus said to the church of Pergamos:

*These things says He who has the sharp two-edged sword: "I know your works, and where you dwell, **where Satan's throne is.** And you hold fast to My name, and did not deny My faith even in the days in which Antipas was My faithful martyr, who was killed among you, **where Satan dwells** (Revelation 2:12–13).*

Though Pergamos was only one city of the Roman Empire, Jesus called it the place where "Satan dwells." On the acropolis above the city, easily visible throughout Pergamos, sat the Pergamon Altar, a giant altar to Zeus with an actual throne—which I believe Jesus referred to as Satan's throne.

In 1886, this altar was dismantled and moved to Berlin, Germany, by a man named Carl Humann. A new museum was built to host this massive display, and it later also hosted a reconstruction of the Ishtar Gate of ancient Babylon. The reconstructed gate of Babylon and the reconstructed Pergamon Altar were finished for the museum's re-opening in 1930, which also happened to be the year Adolf Hitler began his political career. Not long after, the demonic actions of Hitler and the Nazis took history's center stage. I find it hard to believe it a coincidence that Satan's throne was relocated to the same city and in the same year as the beginning of Hitler's career. With these things in mind, I believe Satan's earthly throne was based in Pergamom, then later was moved to Berlin, and eventually will attempt to relocate to the Temple Mount or at least Jerusalem, where the spirit of antichrist will speak through the image of the Beast. Historically, Satan has maintained an earthly throne. To add to the already confusing options about what the Abomination of Desolation might be, here's another idea: Could the Abomination of Desolation be an attempt to relocate the Throne of Zeus again? This time to the Temple Mount? Okay, let's move on.

REVELATION 14:1–8

CAMPING OUT ON MOUNT ZION

Right smack in the middle of the Beast's campaign, Jesus appears on the Earth, on Mount Zion, where He hangs out with the 144,000 Jewish boys who were sealed and protected from all the previous events (see Rev. 14:1). When the apostle John says, right in the midst of Satan's attempted global coup, *"I saw the Lamb standing on Mount Zion"* (Rev. 14:1), I don't believe this event is non-sequential. I think it is play-by- play.

Daniel 7:21–27 gives some added dimension to this view:

I was watching; and the same horn was making war against the saints, and prevailing against them [compare to Rev. 13:7],

until the Ancient of Days came, and a judgment was made in favor of the saints of the Most High, and the time came for the saints to possess the kingdom [compare to Rev. 14:1–7].

Thus he said: "The fourth beast shall be a fourth kingdom on earth, which shall be different from all other kingdoms, and shall devour the whole earth, trample it and break it in pieces. The ten horns are ten kings who shall arise from this kingdom [compare to Rev. 13:1–2].

"And another shall rise after them; He shall be different from the first ones, and shall subdue three kings. He shall speak pompous words against the Most High, shall persecute the saints of the Most High, and shall intend to change times and law. Then the

147

saints shall be given into his hand for a time and times and half a time [compare to Rev. 13:11–18].

"But the court shall be seated, and they shall take away his dominion, to consume and destroy it forever. Then the kingdom and dominion, and the greatness of the kingdoms under the whole heaven, shall be given to the people, the saints of the Most High. His kingdom is an everlasting kingdom, and all dominions shall serve and obey Him" [compare to Rev. 14:6–7] (Daniel 7:21–27).

From this passage, we see that, right in the midst of the Beast nations rise to power and global domination, Heaven steps in. It is that simple. Satan works hard amassing his followers and dominating the world population, but then in a moment, the rightful ruler shows up on the scene, and everything changes.

Jesus lands on Mount Zion and has a pre-triumphant return staff meeting with His 144,000 personal assistants right here on the Earth. From there on out, we see them *"following the Lamb wherever He goes"* (Rev. 14:4). The two witnesses" of Revelation 11 will have already proclaimed the coming King and the coming new temple. So Jesus shows up to spy out the area and hang out with 144,000 of His closest friends.

BABYLON FALLS

The very next section tells us about three angels who fly through the sky making proclamations, the second of which is: *"Babylon is fallen—that great city is fallen..."* (Rev 14:8). This is in the past tense. Since this angelic proclamation is pre-Revelation 17–18, I assume that the decree in Heaven has just been given to release what follows (and is described in Revelation 17:16–17):

And the ten horns which you saw on the beast, these will hate the harlot, make her desolate and naked, eat her flesh and burn her with fire. For God has put it into their heart to fulfill His purpose.

The angel is simply announcing the inevitability of what will soon be carried out in the physical realm in Revelation 17:16. Though more conflict follows, in a very real sense, this is the moment of victory. Jesus stakes His flag (so to speak) on Mount Zion, and from here on out, He maintains control of Earth's battleground. After all, Satan is no match for God.

REVELATION 14:9–13

ANGELIC WARNING

Following the proclamation that Babylon has fallen, and in the wake of the Beast's campaign to implement his "mark" of allegiance, the third angel shouts a warning to the Earth to not take the mark (see Rev. 14:9–11). Because of this urging from the angel, we can assume that there will be non-Christians who refuse to take the mark of the Beast yet survive the Tribulation. After all, what would be the point of warning people not to do it if they didn't really have an option? These non-Christians who resist the Beast will, I believe, be able to walk right into the Millennial Kingdom of Christ even though they are not yet born again.

Don't get me wrong. I am not suggesting that they are automatically *saved* or that they don't need to be. I am simply saying that, logically, some people who have not yet accepted Jesus (but who also didn't worship the Beast) will survive the Tribulation. And there will be babies who are still in their mother's wombs, people who are sick or in comas, and the mentally handicapped. Jesus will not kill them when He returns. Rather, they will have the opportunity to receive His lordship during the thousand-year Kingdom era—an

149

era that will include complete wholeness and heath for all people. This is why the Millennial Kingdom is so important. It provides another grace period.

In the context of the Great Tribulation, we must differentiate between an undecided person and an enemy of Jesus. My theory is based on my understanding of the concept of covenant. If a person isn't an idolater and hasn't taken the mark, but isn't a Christian either, then from a spiritual perspective, that person is still single ("unmarried" to either side). No covenant has yet been made. The point behind the mark of the Beast is to entice the world's population to enter into a covenant with Satan's agenda. This is why the angel's warning clarifies that worshiping the Beast guarantees becoming a recipient of the full strength of God's wrath. This angelic decree reveals another measure of God's grace and patience. The focus is not on being born again, at this point, but just on "staying single." He's saying, "Don't take the mark. If you're not martyred and do survive all this mayhem, you'll have a long time to think about God's offer of covenant. In fact, you'll get to observe Jesus personally."

REVELATION 14:14–16

ANOTHER RAPTURE?

In the midst of the image of the Beast's take-the-mark-or-else campaign, Jesus appears on a cloud with a *"sharp sickle"* (Rev. 14:14) and takes another harvest from the Earth. An angel tells Jesus, *"...The crop on Earth is ripe"* (Rev. 14:15 NLT), so Jesus swings His sickle, and the *"whole earth was harvested"* (Rev. 14:16 NLT). Just when the devil thinks he has Jesus's followers cornered, Jesus pulls off another Rapture, reaching down and pulling them right out of the commotion.

150

Then, immediately after that, another sickle is thrust into the Earth, but this time it is a sickle of judgment (see Rev. 14:17–20). At this point, every believer has been removed from the Earth, and God releases a swift judgment on those who (I assume, based on the warning just prior) were taking the mark (see Rev. 13:9). I find this sequence of events incredible! The demonic image of the Beast implements a system of worship and economy that causes Jesus to respond immediately by taking every believer off the Earth and then crushing Satan's harvest of souls like grapes in a winepress. This particular judgment is depicted as a complete crushing of grapes in a giant winepress. That container is then "trampled outside the city," causing its wine (blood) to spill out onto the land and flow about four feet deep. Whatever this judgment is, it is bloody. The end result is that the image of the Beast doesn't even get the pleasure of being worshipped by his followers.

An interesting event in the book of Joshua can help us visualize what could happen in Revelation 14:17–20. It is the famous battle between the Israelites and the Amorites on the day when the Lord caused the sun to stand still for Joshua. Incidentally, Joshua is the Hebrew name for Jesus.

> So **the LORD routed them before Israel, killed them with a great slaughter** at Gibeon, *chased them along the road that goes to Beth Horon, and struck them down as far as Azekah and Makkedah. And it happened, as they fled before Israel and were on the descent of Beth Horon,* **that the LORD cast down large hailstones from heaven on them** *as far as Azekah, and they died. There were more who died from the hailstones than the children of Israel killed with the sword* (Joshua 10:10–11).

151

In light of this parallel, it appears to me that Heaven itself intervenes and causes a portion of the Beast's army, which is camped around the city of Jerusalem, to be crushed like grapes.

REVELATION 15

THE SONG OF THE LAMB

Now the scene shifts to Heaven, where the people who have just been harvested from the Earth are singing the Song of Moses and the Song of the Lamb—worshipping God (see Rev. 15:2–4). The scene appears to be the very same sea of glass mentioned in Revelation 4:6, only at that point no one was standing on it. Now on the sea of glass *"stood all the people who had been victorious over the beast and his statue and the number representing his name"* (Rev. 15:2 NLT). These are not martyrs who died in the Tribulation; they are those who were *victorious* over the Beast. Like the believers caught up in the first Rapture, these believers had formed a victorious Church in the midst of the Earth's most difficult hour, and after they were harvested from the Earth by Jesus, they were seemingly placed right in front of the throne of God.

Obviously, this group of raptured saints operated in signs and wonders and miracles on the Earth. They were effectively destroying the works of the devil until the Beast was given permission to overcome the saints (see Rev. 13:7). However, Jesus pulls a fast one on the Beast by simply removing the saints from the equation. It is important to note that, prior to that, the saints of the Tribulation were victorious over the Beast. And the song they sing is a song of victory (see Rev. 15:3–4). As the last verse says, *"...for your righteous deeds have been revealed"* (Rev. 15:4).

It is called the Song of Moses and the Song of the Lamb because it is a song of triumph over the attempts of Satan. They rejoice not

152

only because of their victory over Satan's attempts to destroy the saints of the tribulation but also because of God's victories over His enemies even as far back as the Exodus Red Sea crossing. The original song of Moses was a song of victory, and it started out, *"I will sing to the Lord for He has triumphed gloriously"* (Exod. 15:1). It is as if these saints are saying God has never lost a battle; from Exodus until now, He has always been victorious.

At this juncture, we see again that even during the Great Tribulation, the Church is gaining ground. All of Satan's tantrums throughout this series of events are in response to the Lord's initiation of this final battle, which will result in the expulsion of Satan and his demons from the Earth. As Revelation 12:12 says,

Therefore rejoice, O heavens, and you who dwell in them! Woe to the inhabitants of the earth and the sea! For the devil has come down to you, having great wrath, **because he knows that he has a short time.**

Satan is fit to be tied, but Jesus's promise to Peter about the destiny of the Church still stands true:

Blessed are you, Simon Bar-Jonah, for flesh and blood has not revealed this to you, but My Father who is in heaven. And I also say to you that you are Peter, and on this rock I will build My church, and the gates of Hades shall not prevail against it. And I will give you the keys of the kingdom of heaven, and whatever you bind on earth will be bound in heaven, and whatever you loose on earth will be loosed in heaven" (Matthew 16:17–19).

I believe these harvested saints were doing just that—binding, loosing, setting captives free, healing sickness and disease, and raising the dead. They were miraculously feeding multitudes, striking rocks for water, and so forth. They are so powerful that, when Jesus

153

allows the Beast to overpower them, He quickly removes them from the Earth. Otherwise, I suspect they might just re-take the Earth. However, Jesus wants to end this era of Satan's tenancy. He doesn't want a perpetual victorious Church age. He wants the devil, sin, death, and everything else evil completely removed from the equation. If that was not the case, there would be no such thing as the last days. From now on, we should call it "the last days of Satan." They're his last days, not ours! Once Jesus gets His desired harvest from the Earth, He initiates all of the events we read about in Revelation to expedite us toward our eternal state of being. As God has already stated clearly, *"My Spirit will not strive with man forever"* (Gen. 6:3).

The conflict between the Beast and the Lamb is nearly over. The Dragon and the Beast nations have made their bid for world dominion. Yet right in the middle of their campaign, Jesus pulls a sneak attack on Babylon and then takes His stand on Mount Zion. As the image of the Beast is trying to force everyone to take the mark of the Beast, an angel proclaims the penalty of doing so. As the Beast's persecution of and power over the Church intensifies, Jesus snatches them from the Earth in a second Rapture—and then releases judgment on all who took the mark of the Beast. Every time the enemy thinks he's close to winning the upper hand, Jesus steps in and thwarts him. Though they still have a few more battles ahead, at this point, it is clear that the war is already won.

9. Bad Moon Rising

REVELATION 16–19A

We are now peering into the final stages of the Tribulation scenario. A series of seven bowls, each filled with *"the wrath of God"* (Rev. 16:1), are being poured out on the Earth. The wrath of God is an unpopular subject, and it sure doesn't preach very well, but it is God's attitude toward sin, evil, rebellion, and idolatry. These things are at work in the world to undermine His glorious plan and future for His beloved creation. Imagine God as a loving Father who is once and for all dealing with those who are killing His children and refuse to stop. Placed in this context, His wrath—as a Father fighting for His children—is easier to understand. We must put ourselves in God's shoes and ask, *What would I do?*

REVELATION 16

THE BOWLS OF WRATH

My summary of the bowl judgments will be brief. A detailed and exhaustive hypothesis might be interesting, but it would be overly-speculative, too. The important point is clear. God is temporarily making the Earth uninhabitable for those who are attempting to take it over. How this all works out scientifically is unknown. What we do know is that it will happen and that the Earth God created is not for

Satan to enjoy. For this reason, the Lord is making sure that Satan's end-time pseudo-kingdom has no pleasure in it whatsoever. It's like shooting the tires out from under a stolen car. Here are the bullets, in brief:

First Bowl—Malignant sores break out on those who took the mark of the Beast (see Rev. 16:2).

Second Bowl—The seas turn to blood and all the living creatures in them die (see Rev. 16:3).

Third Bowl—The rivers and springs also turn to blood. I assume this is similar to what Moses did in Egypt (see Exod. 7:20).

Fourth Bowl—The sun scorches people with heat; think global warming on steroids (see Rev. 16:8–9).

Fifth Bowl—The Lord drops a supernatural smart bomb right on the throne of the Beast, submerging his kingdom in darkness and pain (see Rev. 16:10–11). Unfortunately for the Beast, his dominion lasts a very short time. The price tags are probably still on the palace furniture.

Sixth Bowl—This bowl is different from the others. The Lord actually paves the way for an international coalition army to cross over the Euphrates River (by drying up the river) so they can gather under the banner of the Beast (see Rev. 16:12–16). The irony is that they are gathering for the sole purpose of doing *"battle against the Lord on that great judgment day of God the Almighty"* (Rev. 16:14 NLT).

Seventh Bowl—Everything that can be shaken is shaken. Thunder, lightening, the greatest of all earthquakes, hail, and significant restructuring of the terrain all accompany Heaven's declaration: *"It is done!"* (see Rev. 16:17–21).

THERE IS NO "BATTLE" OF ARMAGEDDON

Occasionally comments pop up in the news about whether some potentially brewing war could possibly be the Battle of Armageddon. That is wrong thinking and a misunderstanding of Scripture. In fact, there is no Battle of Armageddon; the sixth and seventh bowls clearly show that. A coalition of armies from the Beast nations, what's left of them, gather in the valley of Megiddo to come against the Lord.

Megiddo (Armageddon) is only a gathering place for a meeting of armies coordinated by three frog-like demons that come out of Satan's mouth. The satanic delusion is so strong at this point that the leaders of these nations under Satan's power are literally lambs being led to a slaughter. Satan knows that he *"has a little time"* (Rev. 12:12), and in typical evil fashion, he is placing a human shield between himself and the soon-to-return Jesus Christ. Because Satan knows Scripture, he knows Jesus will be coming from Bozrah, making His way to Jerusalem with His "Joel's army," and he prepares accordingly. (We will cover the details of Christ's return in Chapter 10.)

There is no reversing what is about to happen, and the Lord Himself dries up the Euphrates, as if to say, "Bring it on!" I have often heard it suggested that the drying up of the Euphrates River— so the "kings of the east" can cross over—increases the probability of China getting involved. Maybe they will, and maybe they won't. Iran, Pakistan, and Afghanistan are east of the Euphrates, too. The main point here is that the river is dried up, enabling large military regimes to make their way into Megiddo. I'm sure we will be

157

surprised to discover who turns out. Scripture makes it clear that these armies have been under the influence of a strong web of deceit:

And for this reason God will send them strong delusion, that they should believe the lie, that they all may be condemned who did not believe the truth but had pleasure in unrighteousness (2 Thessalonians 2:11–12).

Of course, the Lord takes no pleasure in the death of the wicked. He is a good God, and His whole purpose in these end-time events is to redeem the rest of His possession from the tenants from hell. This has to happen in order for us to receive our full inheritance and for Jesus to receive His.

It's also important to note that not all of the armies of the world participate in this gathering because many nations will staunchly resist the Beast and the mark throughout the Tribulation. The events here describe Satan's agenda, but not all fall for it. Yes, all have to deal with the cataclysms and the plagues, but the Lord provides for His people and the innocent victims through this time. When Jesus returns, He judges the surviving armies of the Beast in the Valley of Jehoshaphat (see Joel 3:1–2). Then He judges the nations and separates them as one separates the sheep from the goats.

When the Son of Man comes in His glory, and all the holy angels with Him, then He will sit on the throne of His glory. All the nations will be gathered before Him, and He will separate them one from another, as a shepherd divides his sheep from the goats (Matthew 25:31–32).

The sheep nations are those who successfully resisted the Beast. I believe America will be among them, if we are still a nation at that time. As I've said before, this event could be fifty years or five hundred years from now.

As we consider these future events, I want to highlight again the Lord's protection over His people. First, He raptures the existing Church prior to the Tribulation. Following the Rapture, many unbelievers give their hearts to Jesus, forming a new Church on Earth. Though some are martyred, many of them will also be caught up in a second Rapture before things go from bad to worse.

I believe with all my heart that many believers (and possibly even unbelievers who don't worship the Beast) will experience supernatural protection. As Isaiah 3:10–11 says, *Tell the godly all will be well for them. They will enjoy the rich reward they have earned! But the wicked are doomed, for they will get exactly what they deserve* (NLT).

I expect we will meet in Heaven those who refused the mark and chose Jesus in the midst of all this, and they will tell us testimonies of all the supernatural protection and provision they experienced during that time. We get a sneak peak at Jesus's provision for His followers in Revelation 16:15, when He says:

Look I will come as unexpectedly as a thief! Blessed are all who are watching for me, who keep their clothing ready so they will not have to walk around naked and ashamed (NLT).

Here Jesus shoots a personal note into the future, telling those who will worship Him in the midst of the Tribulation to keep their bags packed and their garments on. I believe Jesus is speaking in spiritual terms, using the clothing analogy as a reference to the importance of being aware of their identity and wearing their robes of righteousness. Having said that, Jesus could also be writing to those believers at that time a promise to remove them from the melee also. There is no reason why He wouldn't or couldn't.

LOOKING TOWARD BABYLON

At the pouring out of the seventh bowl, the focus hones in on the mystery city Babylon when a massive earthquake splits the city into three parts (see Rev. 16:18). The views on what this mystery city of Babylon is are diverse. Some believe the ancient city of Babylon will be rebuilt in Iraq. Some say it is Jerusalem, which I believe is a total dereliction of the heart of God and His plans for Israel and Jerusalem. Others, particularly those who believe these events happened in the past, have a difficult time with the idea of a literal mystery city of Babylon.

Along these lines, some say Mystery Babylon was the spirit of pride and religion that controlled humanity through government and religious hierarchy. They claim the beginning of the fall of Mystery Babylon was the rise of Christianity in the early AD 300s, when Constantine became a Christian and made Christianity Rome's official religion, thus beginning what eventually became the Roman Catholic Church.[1]

This interpretation stretches the Revelation 17 timeline approximately 250 years, from Caesar Nero to Constantine. I find this is hard to swallow for many reasons, one of which being the obvious fact that the spirits of pride and religion are alive and well in the world today. If the fall of Babylon is indeed the fall of human pride and its influence in world government, then something has gone haywire. Since then, we have seen such atrocities as the Crusades, the Spanish Inquisition, the rise of Communism, and the Holocaust, not to mention, just two hundred years after Constantine, the birth of the religion of Islam. Since then, Islam has risen to beastly proportions, operating fully under the spirits of human pride and religion and taking these spiritual strongholds to new heights.

160

WHAT AND WHERE IS MYSTERY BABYLON?

I personally fall in with those who believe in a literal future Mystery Babylon, but I am not yet convinced about a particular location.

For now, let's just conclude that, as of today, we don't know for sure where that empire stands; what we do know is that there will be a city that *"rules over the kings of the world"* (Rev. 17:18 NLT). We also know that many believers in this city will be warned to *"Come away from her my people. Do not take part in her sins, or you will be punished with her"* (Rev. 18:4 NLT). This tells me that Mystery Babylon will indeed be a physical city. Otherwise, it makes no sense that the Lord would call His people out. As it was with Sodom, so it will be with Mystery Babylon. To escape the judgment of Sodom, Lot and his family had to leave the city. The same will be true in the future for those who live in Mystery Babylon.

Therefore regardless of the actual location, there is no doubt in my mind that a literal Mystery Babylon will fall in the future. According to what I see in Revelation, it will happen just prior to the triumphant return of Jesus Christ. Flipping ahead a few pages in our Bibles, we see that Revelation 19 starts with the words *after this* and then goes on to describe the heavenly party that happens in response to Mystery Babylon's demise. This hallelujah party then dovetails right into the literal return of our King (see Rev. 19:11). Before we get to that, let's read the saga of the mother of harlots, Mystery Babylon, and her downfall.

REVELATION 17–18

THE NOT SO MYSTERIOUS BABYLON

Mystery Babylon the Great is another hot topic in the Revelation saga. Before I get into who and what Mystery Babylon is in my

161

opinion, I will begin by discussing who and what Mystery Babylon isn't. This list is based on popular mainstream views that I have personally researched over the years, and some of them, at one time or another, I have even considered as the answer.

First, Mystery Babylon is not New York City. Although New York may fit some of the criteria, it does not fit all. Some think that when the twin towers fell on 9-11, it was the fulfillment of Revelation 17 and 18. This is easily refuted because of where the destruction of Babylon fits in the Revelation timeline. It is one of the very last things to happen in the Tribulation. Since I believe the Tribulation is future, New York City and the fall of the twin towers do not fit the description of Mystery Babylon. Plus, I do not believe Mystery Babylon can be located in a predominantly Christian nation. America may have its problems to sort out, but as far as I am concerned, we are still "one nation under God." One of the goals of this book is to inspire this generation to not give up hope for the future of America and the future of the world.

Second, Mystery Babylon is not the Catholic Church. One can purchase books that are four inches thick that have meticulously set out to prove this very thing, but I have some major issues with that view— more than I want to discuss in this chapter. My first and foremost issue with it is that the Catholic Church is Christian. Sure, they have their issues and a history of martyring protestants; I understand that they are a bit overtaken with graven images and a strong emphasis on Mary the mother of Jesus. However, at the very core of Catholicism is the fundamental belief in Jesus Christ, God and Son of God, crucified and risen from the dead. First John 2:22 clearly states, *"Who is a liar but he who denies that Jesus is the Christ? He is antichrist who denies the Father and the Son."* The Catholic Church does not deny the Father or the Son.

In 2007, I was in Guadalajara, Mexico, purchasing furniture and artwork for my import company, The Guadalajara Store. My wife and I toured the massive cathedral in the center of town, Cathedral of the Assumption of Our Lady. The sanctuary was filled with tourists roaming the various altars and vignettes. As we walked through the facility in flow with the crowds, I couldn't help but notice a single worshipper. Sitting in the third row from the front, staring at the massive crucified Jesus up on the platform, was a woman praying with tears flowing down her cheeks. I realized at that moment that, even in the midst of all the gold, pomp, ceremony, statues, and dogma of this massive institution called the Catholic Church, a person can find Jesus. And, in fact, people are free and encouraged to seek Him out. If the Catholic Church was truly the Mystery Babylon Mother of all Harlots, she would provide no path to Jesus. It really is as simple as that. The Mystery Babylon of Revelation is in no way shape or form connected to Christianity. It is, in fact, antithetical to all things Jesus.

Third, Mystery Babylon is not a future global religious system headed up by the Beast nations of the Dragon. As we already discussed, Revelation 13:15–16 makes it clear that humanity will be enticed into worshipping the image of the Beast. This allegiance is proven by the acceptance of some kind of seal or insignia that is proudly displayed on the faithful. Satan's end-time religious agenda is far from a mystery. It is pure and simple idolatry. In fact, it is as simple as it can possibly be—one idol to be worshipped by all people.

Fourth, Mystery Babylon is not Jerusalem. My opinion is so strong against this view that I am even reluctant to discuss it here. However, it is necessary because some are convinced that this is the case. In a nutshell, here's what we must understand: Jesus is not coming to destroy Jerusalem. He is coming to save Jerusalem and establish His throne in it. The Bible makes this clear over and over again throughout the entire Old and New Testament. In the past, Jerusalem has suffered according to prophecy, but the consistent thread throughout God's Word is that it will one day be restored. The following text is just one of the many, many promises of God toward Israel and Jerusalem in the last days.

> *I will bring back the captives of My people Israel. They shall build the waste cities and inhabit them; They shall plant vineyards and drink wine from them; They shall also make gardens and eat fruit from them. I will plant them in their land, And* **no longer shall they be pulled up from the land I have given them,"** *Says the LORD your God* (Amos 9:14–15).

These are four of the predominant views on this subject, all of which I disagree with. Now let me tell you who or better yet *what*, I believe Mystery Babylon is. In the book of Revelation, Mystery Babylon is called a "great city" seven times. One time it is even called a "mighty city" (see Rev. 14:8; 17:18; 18:10,16,18–19,21).

In the field of Bible study, scholars widely use an approach to interpretation called hermeneutics. In this field of study, solid biblical interpretation is held accountable to a variety of criteria. I am going to apply two of these criteria—the principal of first mention and the principal of progressive mention—for the sake of establishing my view. The principal of first mention is based on the idea that the place where a word or concept is first mentioned establishes how that particular subject stands in the mind of God. The principal of progressive mention simply re-affirms that subject as being consistent with its initial introduction into Scripture.

Using these simple criteria, we see that Mystery Babylon is first mentioned in the book of Revelation as a "great city." Afterward, this phrase is consistently repeated without any deviation—with the exception of its third mention, in Revelation 18:10, where it is called a "great city" and a "mighty city." From this we can discern that Mystery Babylon is a city, no question about it. The only mystery about Mystery Babylon is what city and where? Is it a city that exists today? Maybe. Or is it a city that has yet to be built? Maybe. Based on my belief that we have no objective measuring stick to tell us how long it will be until the Church is raptured and the Great Tribulation begins, we cannot know for certain what and where this city is.

Having said that, I believe we can get close to an answer and even speculate with a certain amount of confidence simply due to the fact that Revelation 17 and 18 give us so much information, most of which is keenly descriptive. However, as mentioned throughout this book, the Church's tendency toward *prophetic over-reactionism* has historically left us with egg on our faces. As we read through these chapters, we will get an idea as far as what this city looks like and what kind of location it will sit on. At this point, I will say that I am certain it will be in the Middle East. This is simply because the entire Tribulation scenario epicenter is Jerusalem and the land of Israel. From there, it reaches to the nearby nations then beyond. This is also based on the events directly connected to the triumphant return of Jesus, which I lay out in the following chapter.

REVELATION 17:1–6

BLING AND BLOOD

Right at the beginning of Revelation 17, we are given a large overview of Mystery Babylon. Included in this overview are some geographical indicators. The city sits on "many waters" and is in the "wilderness." This leads me to believe it is a port city that is unique unto itself and that just sort of jumps out of the ground due to its massive scale. After all, it is a "great city." When I lived in Twin

Falls, Idaho, I often drove across the Nevada desert on my way down to Orange County, California, where I grew up. As I approached Las Vegas, I was always impressed with the sheer contrast between the barren desert backdrop and the tall, ultra-modern city. After eight hours of driving through the painted desert of Nevada, the first glance of Las Vegas always caught me by surprise. Don't get me wrong here. Las Vegas is not Mystery Babylon. I simply mention this because I believe this one aspect of Las Vegas helps us visualize the setting John saw.

Another defining characteristic of Mystery Babylon, which is initially introduced as a woman, is that it is decked out in all kinds of *bling*. This is a slang phrase birthed in America's inner cities to describe anything that is over-the-top ornate. Gold teeth, giant diamonds on oversized rings, gold plated wire spoke wheels on a Range Rover, and so forth. You get the picture.

The less attractive side of the city includes the fact that it is *"drunk with the blood of the saints and with the martyrs of Jesus..."* (Rev. 17:6). This tells us that this city is not Christian-friendly at all. We know that in the beginning a Christian community will exist within its walls because in Revelation 18:4 a voice from Heaven says, *"Come out of her my people...."* In the end, this city will be a known place of Christian martyrdom. In fact, I believe it may be the place where many believers of the Tribulation will be sent to be executed.

REVELATION 17:7–18

MYSTERY BABYLON AND THE BEAST

Now things get a bit technical in regard to the structure and the hierarchy of the Beast nations and their relationship with Mystery

Babylon. For the sake of not getting bogged down here, I will be broad in my descriptions.

A. The city described as a woman is carried by the Beast nations (see Rev. 17:7). Therefore, I conclude that this city is supported and funded by these nations.

B. The founders and the rulers of this city are of one mind with the Beast nations. They are allies in cause and purpose. The city subsequently takes orders from the leaders of the Beast nations as they together come against Jesus Christ and His people (see Rev. 17:13–14).

C. In a surprising turn of events, the Beast nations turn on the city and destroy it, thus bringing about the destruction of the great city Mystery Babylon. My suspicion is that this great city's influence on the nations may be overshadowing the other ten nations that make up the coalition of Beast nations, which causes them to destroy it (see Rev. 17:16–18). REVELATION 18:1–8

A Luxurious Obsession

At the beginning of Revelation 18, we read some more telling details about the obsession this city has with luxury and opulence. Its high-end lifestyle has made the "merchants of the earth" very rich. I believe this city's appeal will be more than most business people can resist. I doubt that any vendor or supplier will be technically judged by God for dealing with this city, but in the end, they will lose their cash cow. As mentioned previously, many of God's people will be living in this city until the time of its appointed destruction. I suspect many secret Christians and Christians-in-hiding within the catacombs of this massive complex will find their way out prior to its impending doom. I am excited to hear, in Heaven, the miraculous testimonies from those who lived through it of angels guiding people out, prison doors opening, and guards being unable to see believers walking right past them.

REVELATION 18:9–24

IN ONE HOUR

In the next passage, we see the magnitude of the destruction of this city and get an idea of its logistics. In verses 17–19 it says that those who *"travel by ship, sailors, and as many as trade on the sea"* will cry over the city's destruction. I am imagining merchants standing on the decks of their large freighters filled with SUVs, Jet Skis, furniture, and the like; though they are miles away, they can see the great pummels of smoke coming from the city that was their destination. Large manufacturing firms will be calculating the cost in their heads as they receive messages from the freight delivery companies that they are turning the ships around with massive cargos undelivered.

It's also important to notice how quickly the city falls. Those who mourn the city's destruction cry out, *"...For in one hour your judgment has come"* (Rev. 18:10). We can only speculate as to how this city will fall, though the obvious first thought that comes to my mind is a nuclear explosion. After all, verse 8 says, *"She will be utterly burned with fire."* And Revelation 17:16 says, *"And the ten horns which you saw on the beast, these will hate the harlot, make her desolate and naked, eat her flesh and burn her with fire."* Though we don't see all the specifics, the outcome is clear—and it's not a pretty one.

Ultimately, when this city is judged and destroyed, it is completely wiped out. Nothing will be left! In combination, the basic tenets of this city—global enterprise, sorcery, and Christian persecution—reaped eternal judgment from God. It will never be rebuilt.

SATAN'S "WIFE"

Now I want to discuss the role and purpose of Mystery Babylon in the end-times Satanic pseudo-empire. In Revelation 21:9, we discover that the New Jerusalem is called the Lamb's wife. As strange as it may seem, the manifest body of Jesus's wife takes the form of a city, New Jerusalem. Somehow this city and our relationship to it, by occupancy and interaction, complete the bride of Christ. Conversely, the mystery city of Babylon will be Satan's imitation New Jerusalem. In his attempt to rob Jesus of His full reward, he even tries to duplicate the bride of Christ in all of her nuances and complexities. When we scan over Revelation 17 and 18, we can see that God calls this city a decadent, drunken whore (see Rev. 17:4–5). Yet she calls herself a queen (see Rev. 18:7). And interestingly, in the Scriptures, Babylon is always referred to as *she*.

Thus we can see that the antithesis of Babylon is the New Jerusalem, who is clothed in the righteousness of the saints (see Rev. 19:18). She rests on the foundation of the twelve apostles (see Rev. 21:14)—a significant contrast to Mystery Babylon, who is the *"mother of harlots and of the abominations"* (Rev. 17:5). After her destruction, Babylon will never be lit with even so much as a lamp again (see Rev. 18:23), but the New Jerusalem will be forever lit by the presence of God, and it will never be defiled or host any abomination (see Rev. 21:22–27).

In light of all this, I am intrigued by the fact that the Beast nations, who are controlled by the Dragon (Satan), actually turn on this city and destroy her (see Rev. 17:16). However, when we consider the very nature of evil itself, we can see that this would have to be the case. The very kingdom of Satan is actually imploding on itself. God easily dismantles Satan's agenda by causing his own cohorts to turn on him and destroy his bride. *"For God has put it into their hearts to fulfill His purpose..."* (Rev. 17:17).

Now that the Lord has cleared the Earth of the detestable whore, Mystery Babylon, we move on to the next event—the wedding celebration of the Lamb.

REVELATION 19:1–10

THE MARRIAGE SUPPER OF THE LAMB

As we've seen in Revelation 16–18, the destruction of Satan's capital city and bride, Mystery Babylon, is complete. The war is nearly over; now it is time for the grand finale of all history—the triumphant return of Jesus Christ and the final defeat of Satan and his army.

As Mystery Babylon crashes to the ground, a vast crowd in Heaven cheers and affirms the righteous judgments of God. After thousands of years of God's redemptive process, a new era has begun on Earth. It is time for the physical cohabitation of God and humanity on this Earth. Jesus Christ, the one who is faithful and true, is ready to come and make war against the armies of the Beast and claim His prize because of His desire to be with us.

The apostle Paul wrote about this future hope in First Corinthians 13:12: *For now we see through a glass, darkly; but then face to face: now I know in part; but then shall I know even as also I am known* (KJV).

As Heaven celebrates, a multitude of voices announces a very important event within the advent of Christ's return—the Marriage Supper of the Lamb (see Rev. 19:7). As I understand it, we believers will be attendants of this feast. Based on where this event lands in the text, I believe the marriage supper happens between the destruction of Mystery Babylon and the triumphant return of Jesus. The dinner is before the wedding. I haven't heard or read a strong, objective commentary on the details of the wedding feast beyond the obvious facts of proper attire and the importance of being there. As Revelation 19:9 says, *"Blessed are those who are invited to the wedding feast of the Lamb"* (NLT). The point seems to be that Jesus is about to go claim His bride. And if we are at this supper, then the question is: *Who is the bride?*

At this point, I am going to make a confession: I do not fully understand the Church/Bride analogy. I know I am in good company because most of my favorite preachers and teachers frequently use disclaimers when talking about the Bride of Christ. Even the apostle Paul called it a *"great mystery"* in Ephesians 5:32. However, it is an important part of the New Testament and the Revelation timeline, not to mention our identity in Christ.

As we discussed briefly before, in Revelation 21:9, an angel introduces John to the *"wife of the Lamb."* Since she is called His wife, I assume this means they are already married. The wife is then revealed as the *"holy city, Jerusalem, descending out of heaven from God."* In Revelation 19:8, it also says of her: "And *to her was granted that she should be arrayed in fine linen, clean and white: for the fine linen is the righteousness of saints"* This statement differentiates her from the saints. The question is: *Can a city be a wife?* As we just discussed, the storyline of Revelation also contains a counterfeit city wife—Mystery Babylon. Considering all these details, it seems that a city can become a wife. This is mind-boggling. To make matters even more complicated, the apostle Paul calls the New Jerusalem the *"mother of us all"* (Gal. 4:26).

171

The Church/Bride analogy baffles me. Praise God the dim glass will be removed one day, and we will know all the answers. What we do know now is this: There is a Bride, and we are somehow part of the relationship between Christ and His Bride; and there will be a wedding feast, and blessed are all who are at that party.

THE TESTIMONY OF JESUS

The one thing I am not perplexed about is Jesus, my Lord and savior. This portion of Revelation 19 closes with a surprising event involving Jesus's lordship and the power of the testimony. After seeing and hearing the prophecy of Revelation, the apostle John is so moved that, in a moment of awe and passion, he falls down in worship of the messenger angel. However, the angel quickly puts a stop to it, saying, *"Worship only God!"* (Rev 19:10 NLT). I can only imagine the shock and fear that angel may have felt. The last angel (Lucifer) who wanted to receive worship from God's people didn't fare so well.

The angel concludes his admonition to John with this intriguing statement: *"For the testimony of Jesus is the spirit of prophecy"* (Rev. 19:10). This statement made by the angel has huge implications in the world today. It tells us that the when the acts of God are told and declared that the power of God is released to perform them. Even today, when we repeat the things that God has done, healing miracles, supernatural provision and such; in essence we are prophesying that He will do it again. Those that hear the testimony can take hold of it in faith and become recipients of the same miracles in their own life. John's emotional state of awe causes him to react inappropriately in the moment. He is softly rebuked and encouraged to stay in prophecy mode. He must stay focused, for he has much to prophesy to the nations regarding what he's already seen

172

and the victorious arrival of his merciful warrior king, which is coming up next.

10. The Merciful Warrior King

REVELATION 19

Now we get to the best part! Unfortunately, many have decided that the details of Christ's return aren't important as long as we know He is coming. I disagree. Not only is Jesus our healer and the salvation of our very beings, but He is the victorious warrior and the coming King! This chapter is my attempt to examine that aspect of my Jesus. I love all of Him—including the warrior part. It is a part of Him many believers don't like to think about, but we must remember that this part of His nature is reserved for Satan and all who purposely and willingly have chosen to stand with him until the end. The book of Revelation is titled, in its original Greek, *Apocalypto*. In English, we say *Apocalypse*. It simply means "to reveal or unveil something."1 The book of Revelation is a full disclosure of Jesus Christ—in His goodness, in His fairness, in His mercy, in His deity, and in His wrath. This full unveiling culminates in the triumphant Final Return of Jesus Christ, which follows all of the events of the Great Tribulation. When He comes, His wrath will be aimed precisely at the armies of the Beast and the False Prophet and all who received the mark of the Beast. As we know, the Church is with Jesus, so His primary mission at His return is to reclaim Jerusalem and establish His thousand-year earthly Kingdom.

Eventually this will morph into a permanent and infinite Kingdom and a multi-dimensional reality—an era when there will be no veil or dim glass that we must discern through. It will be an era of bliss and eternal increase and the expansion of realms that we are not yet aware of.

HE COMES TO SAVE

But the first step is reclaiming Earth. When He does this, I believe that no innocent bystanders or children will be harmed. Although many will suffer in the Tribulation, I believe that, upon His return, He will supernaturally protect all of the innocent. Satan's typical ploy— using human shields—will have no effect. As I've discussed already, I believe God will continually evangelize the lost throughout the Great Tribulation and even during the Millennial Kingdom. We will see this again as we progress through the events of Jesus's return in Revelation 19. His only enemies at His return will be those who have willfully decided to be His enemies. There is nothing even He can do about that. Yet even in His wrath, He is full of grace, and He is always good.

This is a very crucial and pivotal position in my eschatology: Jesus is not coming to destroy but to save. If we back up a few chapters, we see the foundation for God's judgments clearly laid out by the angelic announcements of Revelation 14:

Then I saw another angel flying in the midst of heaven, having the everlasting gospel to preach to those who dwell on the earth—to every nation, tribe, tongue, and people— saying with a loud voice, "Fear God and give glory to Him, for the hour of His judgment has come; and worship Him who made heaven and earth, the sea and springs of water" (Revelation 14:6–7).

176

As the moment of judgment looms, God sends forth an angel to plead with people to turn their hearts to Him so that they can be saved. Then, after an angelic announcement that Satan's kingdom has come crashing down (see Rev. 14:8), a third angel follows with a warning to the people of the Earth that they should not align themselves with the Beast and the False Prophet:

Then a third angel followed them, saying with a loud voice, "If anyone worships the beast and his image, and receive his mark on his forehead or on his hand, he himself shall also drink of the wine of the wrath of God, which is poured out full strength into the cup of His indignation (Revelation 14:9–10).

This is a clear indication that Jesus will not destroy all people who are not born again at His coming, but only those who have accepted the mark of the Beast by embracing his satanic ideology and making a conscious decision to align themselves with the plan and the will of the Beast and the False Prophet.

Jesus will come to destroy the nations who have aligned themselves with Satan's evil agenda against Israel—specifically the leaders and the armies of those nations. With great precision, He will destroy those who are foolish enough to willfully join in the campaign against the Son of God. Even though they have been through all of the terrible events of the Great Tribulation, their hearts have remained hard and unrepentant. (Having said that, as we will see later in this chapter, even many of the soldiers of the Beast's army will survive and will be judged by Christ Himself in the Valley of Jehoshaphat). Thus, we can clearly see that the Day of Vengeance is specifically addressed toward Satan and his followers, not toward all of humanity.

THE DAY OF VENGEANCE

When Jesus came to His hometown of Nazareth, He went into the synagogue and read aloud from Isaiah 61:1–2a:

> *"The Spirit of the LORD is upon Me, because He has anointed Me to preach the gospel to the poor; He has sent Me to heal the brokenhearted, To proclaim liberty to the captives and recovery of sight to the blind, to set at liberty those who are oppressed; To proclaim the acceptable year of the LORD."* **Then He closed the book, and gave it back to the attendant and sat down.** *And the eyes of all who were in the synagogue were fixed on Him. And He began to say to them,* **"Today this Scripture is fulfilled in your hearing."** *So all bore witness to Him, and marveled at the gracious words which proceeded out of His mouth...* (Luke 4:18–22).

When He did this, Jesus proclaimed His mission for His life on Earth based on Isaiah's prophecy of the coming Messiah. However, it is important to note that He did not read the entire passage. Rather, He stopped right in the middle of a verse; I believe He did it on purpose and for a significant reason. When Jesus stopped reading and said, *"Today this scripture is fulfilled in your hearing,"* He was telling us what He would do while on Earth—as well as what He wouldn't do until later, at His Final Return. Here's what Isaiah wrote that Jesus left out:

> **And the day of vengeance of our God;** *to comfort all who mourn, to console those who mourn in Zion, to give them beauty for ashes, the oil of joy for mourning, the garment of praise for the spirit of heaviness; that they may be called trees of righteousness, the planting of the LORD, that He may be glorified." And they shall rebuild the old ruins, they shall raise up the former*

desolations, and they shall repair the ruined cities, the desolations of many generations (Isaiah 61:2b—4).

I believe Jesus stopped at that particular point in the prophecy because the rest of it was (and still is) yet to come. In other words, Jesus was not yet walking in the fulfillment of the rest of the prophecy, which speaks of *"the day of vengeance"* and the restoration of the nation of Israel, *"to console those who mourn **in Zion."***

Currently we are living in the era of the *continued* fulfillment of what Jesus claimed on that day in Nazareth in the synagogue. I can say with confidence today that

The Spirit of the LORD is upon Me, because He has anointed Me to preach the gospel to the poor; He has sent Me to heal the brokenhearted, to proclaim liberty to the captives and recovery of sight to the blind, to set at liberty those who are oppressed; to proclaim the acceptable year of the LORD.

But I cannot claim the following statement—"and *the day of vengeance of our God."* That portion of the Isaiah prophecy is not mine to claim or declare. Jesus Christ will return to finish the job Himself. He will personally destroy Satan. Though the Church will be successful, on many fronts, at destroying the works of Satan, we cannot dislodge Him from this Earth. We also cannot clear the core of the Earth and the second heaven of the demons that are roaming loose. This is Jesus's job, which He will accomplish at His Final Return, along with an army of angels and resurrected saints. He will pick up in Isaiah 61 where He left off on that historic day in the Nazareth synagogue.

REVELATION 19:11–16

THE MOMENT OF BREAKTHROUGH

Now let's look at the specifics of what will happen when Jesus returns to accomplish the day of vengeance. From Revelation 1:7, we know how He will come:

> *Behold, He is coming with clouds, and every eye will see Him, even they who pierced Him. And all the tribes of the earth will mourn because of Him. Even so, Amen.*

In other words, Jesus will present Himself to the world with an open Heaven view for all to see. John reinforces this in Revelation 19 as well, saying, *"I saw heaven opened, and a white horse was standing there. Its rider was named Faithful and True..."* (Rev. 19:11 NLT). This is the same name that Jesus attributes to Himself in Revelation 3:14. John continues by describing Jesus in His triumphant battle array, giving a much different presentation than the one in Revelation 5:6, where Jesus is the Lamb who had been slain. To us (His followers), Jesus is the Lamb of God. To Satan and His ragtag army, Jesus is the conquering King whose *"eyes were like flames of fire, and on His head were many crowns"* (Rev. 19:12 NLT).

The Beast has seven heads with ten crowns, but they are crowns without a kingdom. It is a complete sham. Jesus Himself is wearing the crown of the Kingdom of Heaven, and on the day of vengeance, He will be bringing His Kingdom to this world. This reminds me of an episode from the hit comedy television series, *The Office* (USA), in which Dwight is pulled over by a policeman for impersonating an officer with his counterfeit police light on his car. He posed as a police officer, but then he is dealt with by a real officer. Likewise, this event in Revelation 19 is the return of the real King, and the fake one is about to be incarcerated.

REVELATION 19:17–21

WITH GREAT PRECISION

In anticipation of what is to follow, an angel summons the scavenger birds to gather and await the "feast" that is about to follow. But, in fact, no actual battle happens. Passages like Daniel 10:13 tell of how Michael the Archangel had to battle the demon prince over Persia for twenty-one days to open the way for a messenger angel to get to Daniel, but this is not that. Jesus is not an angel. He is God-made-flesh, and in His presence, Satan has zero chance. Yet he still gathers his army and comes, deluded by his own pride:

And I saw the beast, the kings of the earth, and their armies, gathered together to make war against Him who sat on the horse and against His army (Revelation 19:19).

This is mind-boggling to me, yet we know this kind of hard heartedness exists. The story of the Pharaoh of Egypt in the book of Exodus is a prime example of such evil persistence. He allowed himself and his people to suffer through plague after plague—to the point of undeniable proof that the God of Israel had power over him and all of creation—yet, he insisted on hardening his heart against God and God's people. He even convinced an army to follow after the children of Israel and attempt to overtake them in the desert. The Egyptian men in this army had all suffered through the plagues brought on by Moses and Aaron. They had seen rivers turned to blood, frogs covering the entire land, locusts devouring their crops, and even the death of every firstborn male, including livestock. Yet they still mustered up enough hatred and disdain for God and His people to ride right into the Red Sea while it was supernaturally divided by God Himself.

It is this kind arrogance and defiance that exists within the human race that, in the end, Jesus Christ will remove from this Earth. He will do it with an unprecedented display of supernatural strength and righteousness, and He will execute this judgment with surgical precision. This is the purpose of His sword:

Now out of His mouth goes a sharp sword, that with it He should strike the nations (Revelation 19:15).

The psalmist David speaks of the mighty power of the voice of God:

To Him who rides on the heaven of heavens which were of old! Indeed, He sends out His voice, a mighty voice. Ascribe strength to God; His excellence is over Israel, and His strength is in the clouds (Psalm 68:33–34).

And the author of Hebrews tells us of the precision of God's Word.

For the word of God is living and powerful, and sharper than any two-edged sword, piercing even to the division of soul and spirit, and of joints and marrow, and is a discerner of the thoughts and intents of the heart. And there is no creature hidden from His sight, but all things are naked and open to the eyes of Him to whom we must give account (Hebrews 4:12–13).

These three verses paint a picture of the power and the precision that Jesus can and will execute in His judgment at His return. All the destruction will happen by the sheer command of His word, carried by the very sound waves He creates. As Hebrews 4:13 confirms, there is no escaping Him.

Thus, without a battle, the Beast and the False Prophet are immediately captured and thrown into the lake of fire (see Rev. 19:20). From the moment the "battle" begins, the army is without its leaders. Then, when Jesus shouts, anyone within an earshot of His voice is instantly killed unless they surrender. I assume they will plug their ears as they flee, as Isaiah 2:21 tells us: *"...They will try to escape the terror of the Lord and the glory of His majesty as He rises to shake the earth"* (NLT). This is the beginning of the so-called Battle of Armageddon. Not all the armies of the Beast have been dealt with yet. From this time forward, it will take Jesus and His army a number of days to make their way from Bozrah to Jerusalem. In fact, the entire campaign could take as long as forty-five days from the moment Jesus appears in the clouds (see Rev. 19:11) until He establishes His throne in Jerusalem.2

VENGEANCE ROAD

However, because Revelation's coverage of this event is fairly short, I also want to examine several Old Testament prophecies that give us some additional important details concerning God's Day of Vengeance and what is possibly the literal path of the Lords return on earth. In his prophecies about the end-times, Joel described the Lord's army like this:

A fire devours before them, and behind them a flame burns; the land is like the Garden of Eden before them, and behind them a desolate wilderness; surely nothing shall escape them. Their appearance is like the appearance of horses; and like swift steeds, so they run. With a noise like chariots over mountaintops they leap, like the noise of a flaming fire that devours the stubble, like a strong people set in battle array (Joel 2:3–5).

As previously highlighted, I am convinced that the impact of His army is the direct result of the voice of Jesus Christ. He is now displaying the raw power of the spoken word when it is in full submission to the will of the Father.

FIRST STOP BOZRAH

The prophet Isaiah, who also spoke of the day of God's vengeance, saw Jesus coming from Bozrah of Edom. Bozrah was an ancient city near the rock city of Petra (which I mentioned earlier as the possible refuge city for Israel during the Great Tribulation). Edom was the ancient name for that entire region, which was once inhabited by the Edomites.

In Revelation 12:6 it says, *"And the woman fled into the wilderness, where God had prepared a place to care for her for 1260 days."* At that time, I believe the people will flee to Edom. However, it would be safe to assume that many of them may have scattered in the wilderness along the way.

In the following verses, Isaiah dialogues with Jesus about what He has been doing in Bozrah:

ISAIAH: *Who is this who comes from Edom, from the city of Bozrah, with his clothing stained red? Who is this in royal robes, marching in his great strength?*

JESUS: *It is I, the LORD, announcing your salvation! It is I, the LORD, who has the power to save!*

ISAIAH: *Why are your clothes so red, as if you have been treading out grapes?*

JESUS: *I have been treading the winepress alone; no one was there to help me. In my anger I have trampled my enemies as if they were grapes. In my fury I have trampled my foes. Their blood has stained my clothes. For the time has come for me to avenge my people, to ransom them from their oppressors. I was amazed to see that no one intervened to help the oppressed. So I myself stepped in to save them with my strong arm, and my wrath sustained me. I crushed the nations in my anger and made them stagger and fall to the ground, spilling their blood upon the earth.*

ISAIAH: *I will tell of the LORD's unfailing love. I will praise the LORD for all he has done. I will rejoice in his great goodness to Israel, which he has granted according to his mercy and love.*

JESUS: *They are my very own people. Surely they will not betray me again.*

ISAIAH: *And he became their Savior. In all their suffering he also suffered, and* **he personally rescued them** (Isaiah 63:1–9 NLT).

Based on this sequence of verses in Isaiah and the sequence of the book of Revelation, it appears that Jesus's first stop on Earth will be Edom, where He will rescue the Jews and any others who have been refugees there. From there, Jesus and His Heavenly Army (and possibly the 144,000) will make their way to Jerusalem to reclaim the Holy City and Mount Zion as Jesus's dwelling place. As Isaiah 4:4–5 prophesies:

The Lord will wash the filth from beautiful Zion and cleanse Jerusalem from its bloodstains with the hot breath of fiery judgment. Then the Lord will provide shade for Mount Zion and all who assemble there (NLT).

FROM EDOM TO ZION

From Edom Jesus and His entourage will make their way to Jerusalem. And it will be no small affair.

> *For as the lightning comes from the east and flashes to the west, so also will the coming of the Son of Man be. For wherever the carcass is, there the eagles will be gathered together.* (Matt 24:27-28)

Here is an idea. As Jesus and His entourage make their way to Zion across the desert, their coming will be seen from a distance. It will literally appear like a lightning storm coming toward Jerusalem (see Joel 2:3–5). And in the wake of this campaign across the desert, which results in a complete destruction of the enemy armies, the birds circle in the air as they feast on the carnage. This fits perfectly with the angelic invitation to the birds to *"Come! Gather together for the great banquet God has prepared. Come and eat the flesh of kings..."* (Rev. 19:17–18 NLT).

ON TO THE MOUNT OF OLIVES

From Edom, Jesus and His entourage go straight to the Mount of Olives, which overlooks Jerusalem, and more specifically, to the Temple Mount, which is also called Mount Zion. The prophet Zechariah gives a brief mention of Jesus's battle against the nations of the Beast, noting that He ultimately will make His way to the Mount of Olives. His very presence on the Mount of Olives will cause it to split in half.

> *Then the LORD will go out to fight against those nations, as he has fought in times past. On that day his feet will stand on the Mount of Olives, east of Jerusalem. And the Mount of Olives will split apart, making a wide valley running from east to west. Half*

the mountain will move toward the north and half toward the south. You will flee through this valley, for it will reach across to Azal. Yes, you will flee as you did from the earthquake in the days of King Uzziah of Judah. Then the LORD my God will come, and all his holy ones with him (Zechariah 14:3–5 NLT).

The view from the Mount of Olives onto the Temple Mount is by far the best vantage point from which to view the city of Jerusalem. A series of bus parking zones are situated along that road, and every single day, hundreds of tourists unload there to take pictures of the Temple Mount and the east gate of Jerusalem. Between the Mount of Olives and the Temple Mount is also the Garden of Gethsemane, where Jesus agonized and was arrested to be crucified. From this same hill, Jesus will descend onto the Temple Mount.

The prophet Zechariah also tells us what the conditions in Jerusalem will be when Christ returns.

Watch, for the day of the LORD is coming when your possessions will be plundered right in front of you! I will gather all the nations to fight against Jerusalem. The city will be taken, the houses looted, and the women raped. Half the population will be taken into captivity, and the rest will be left among the ruins of the city (Zechariah 14:1–2 NLT).

ON INTO THE CITY

Jesus and His army now make their way from the Mount of Olives right through the surrounding homes and buildings on to the Temple Mount. The prophet Joel gives some pretty amazing detail of this event. Here are some of the highlights:

Sound the alarm in Jerusalem! Raise the battle cry on my holy mountain. Let everyone tremble in fear because the day of the

Lord is upon us. Suddenly like dawn spreading across the mountains, a great and mighty army appears. Nothing like it has been seen before or will ever be seen again (Joel 2:1–2 NLT).

The attackers march like warriors and scale city wall like soldiers. Straight forward they march never breaking rank. They never jostle each other; each moves in exactly the right position. They break through defenses without missing a step. They swarm over the city and run along its walls. They enter all the houses climbing like thieves through the windows. The earth quakes as they advance, and the heavens tremble. The Lord is at the head of the column. He leads them with a shout. This is His mighty army, and they follow His orders... (Joel 2:7–11 NLT).

It goes without saying that Jesus and His army will swiftly reclaim Jerusalem as His own. Yet even on this Day of Vengeance, Jesus will evangelize as He goes. We see this in Joel 2:12–14; immediately following His entrance into Jerusalem, He will say:

Turn to Me now, while there is time. Give me your hearts. Come with fasting, weeping and mourning. Don't tear your clothing in grief, but tear your hearts instead. Return to the Lord your God, for he is merciful and compassionate, slow to anger and filled with unfailing love. He is eager to relent and not punish. Who knows, perhaps he will give you a reprieve, sending you a blessing instead of curse.

This part of Joel's prophecy really shows the goodness of God. Even as He is returning in full battle array, Jesus will be shouting ahead offering amnesty for those who will surrender. I suspect there will be many takers. This tactic of offering grace to those who would surrender has been commonly used in warfare throughout all of history. If people, who are born in sin, are often willing to show mercy to those who surrender, we know that Jesus Christ will be even quicker to offer mercy. No doubt this will result in another great harvest for the Kingdom. Honestly, I think the attempted implementation of the mark of the Beast will be a hard sell, and Satan's turnout won't be as high as he hopes.

THE ULTIMATE REVIVAL

So many, when reading Revelation, view the end-times as a very dark and hopeless time. And no doubt it is. But they focus solely on the terror of evil rather than the glory of God and the new Kingdom He will introduce. I prefer to think of the conclusion of the end-times as the ultimate revival. As I mentioned previously, in Acts 2 we learn that, like Peter, we can draw on a future promise and gain a portion now. Peter claimed Joel 2:28—"Then *after these things, I will pour out My spirit upon all people*"—*for* his day, even though he didn't experience the fullness of it. I believe a greater fulfillment of this passage awaits the Church prior to the Rapture, and I believe the greatest fulfillment of this passage will happen at the return of Jesus Christ, when He has rescued Jerusalem from the Beast, the False Prophet, and the people who were foolish enough to fall for their ploy.

When Jesus and His army take Jerusalem, the Earth will experience an unprecedented outpouring of the Holy Spirit, and we will be drunk with new wine in the presence of Jesus Christ. The whole world will be laughing, rolling on the floor, and having a blast as we jump for joy. I can't even begin to imagine the magnitude of this outpouring. Up until this point, the world has already experienced great outpourings and revivals. Billions of souls have come into the Kingdom prior to Christ's return, but with God there's always more! Isn't it just like Jesus to serve the best wine last?

JUDGING THE ARMIES

After the outpouring of the Holy Spirit, the only remaining piece left in Jesus's mission is to judge the enemy armies. Joel 3:2 tells us about this: *"I will gather the armies of the world in the valley of Jehoshaphat. There I will judge them for harming my people and my special possession..."* (NLT). Here, the Hebrews phrase translated as *valley of Jehoshaphat* is a locative noun. In other words, it is an actual location. *Strong's Concordance* describes it as the valley between the Mount of Olives and Jerusalem.3 It is a rather narrow ravine, but its length reaches for miles, all the way to the Dead Sea. So this is doable. As far as I can tell, this is Jesus first order of business as King on this Earth. He judges the armies of the Beast.

From this passage, we know there will be survivors from the opposing side. However, I am sure the defection rate will be at its highest ever. Revelation 1:7 tells us, *"Behold, He is coming with clouds, and every eye will see Him, even they who pierced Him. **And all the tribes of the earth will mourn because of Him."*** At the first appearance of Jesus in the clouds, I am sure many of these soldiers will repent as they are changing their britches. It is uncertain whether they will all have the mark of the Beast. Revelation 13:16 says, *"And he causeth all, both small and great, rich and poor, free and bond, to receive a mark in their right hand, or in their foreheads"* (KJV). The word translated *causeth* in Greek is *poieo,* which means he set a decree or a law in motion.4 It is his plan and desire, but we have no way of knowing how successful Satan will be at pulling it off. He won't have very much time, and as we discussed earlier, in Revelation 14:17–20, a huge portion of his workforce will be wiped out in an instant. Many soldiers will flee, while others who are being deployed from other parts of the world just won't show up. Some might accuse me of reading into the text. I am. I am assuming that

Jesus is full of grace and mercy and that Satan is a loser. From that position, I interpret Scripture.

After the "battle" is over, Jesus will round them all up, everyone to the Valley of Jehoshaphat. At this judgment, I assume Revelation 14:9–10 will be enforced and carried out:

Anyone who worships the beast and his statue or who accepts his mark on their forehead or on the hand must drink the wine of God's anger. It has been poured full strength into the cup of God's wrath. And they will be tormented with fire and burning sulfur in the presence of the holy angels and the Lamb (NLT).

At the very least, the decree will be pronounced over them at this time, but some may be spared because they didn't take the mark. In the following chapter, we will get another glimpse of this court scenario. Because of the sheer quantity of cases, the Lord will immediately put us to work, appointing us to our roles as kings and priests.

Up to this point, we have traced the path of Jesus from His open Heaven revealing to His ground exploits—from Bozrah, then across the desert to the Mount of Olives, and then into Jerusalem. Satan's free reign on this Earth has expired, and Jesus has assumed His role as King of this Earth in the flesh.

With that, humanity is headed into what will become the golden era of planet Earth as we know it. Jesus will teach us how this world was designed to work, and He will unlock mysteries that we didn't know existed. I assume the entire infrastructure of most major cities will be upgraded. A supernatural lifestyle will be had by all. Technology will advance at unprecedented levels. Many of the projects started by the Church of the end-times will be picked back up and finished. Desert lands will be flowing with water. Agricultural technologies will be implemented. Housing will boom, and new cities and kingdoms will be established. Artistic communities will buzz with creativity and advancement in every arena. One of the most provocative realities of this thousand-year dominion is that those who are in their resurrected glorified bodies will interact with people who are in their natural bodies, just as Jesus did for forty days after His resurrection.

11. The Sequel

REVELATION 20

Imagine going to the movies. The film is an epic battle between good and evil. After an intense series of fights and chase scenes, the final showdown happens. This, of course, takes place in a multi-level abandoned warehouse that just so happens to have all the electricity on, the conveyor belts running, giant hooks hanging, and plenty of empty metal barrels stacked and ready to fall over. The villain is finally captured, and the movie ends with his incarceration. Society breathes a sigh of relief. But as you leave the theater, you have a sneaking suspicion that there will be a sequel. Somehow, some day the villain will escape that prison or his sentence will expire, and he will be released once again. Of course, he hasn't forgotten his old foe—which leads to another huge box office success in the making. We've seen it over and over on the big screen. At the end of time, we'll see it in history. Welcome to Revelation 20, the sequel above all sequels.

REVELATION 20:1–3

THE INCARCERATION OF SATAN

As in this movie scenario, at the end of the greatest battle between good and evil, Satan—the villain of all villains—is bound and locked in the bottomless pit for a thousand years. However, we know it's not over. It's not just a feeling, either. The Bible clearly says it:

The angel threw him into the bottomless pit, which he then shut and locked so Satan could not deceive the nations anymore until the thousand years were finished. Afterward he must be released for a little while (Revelation 20:3 NLT).

Jesus has returned and dealt with the Beast and the False Prophet of the Great Tribulation. Their campaign ends forever in the lake of fire, and there will be no sequel for them. However, in His infinite wisdom, God has decided that Satan will serve a thousand-year sentence and then be released for a brief time.

I believe this pit is actually the center of the Earth. I'm not a scientist, but I imagine that if we drilled a hole all the way through the Earth, from one side to the other, and then jumped into the hole, we would free-fall all the way to the center. There we would be suspended due to the force of gravity pulling in both directions. I assume a natural body would disintegrate, but a spiritual body is different. Satan has a spiritual body. One reason why I'm convinced this bottomless pit is actually the core of the Earth is found in Revelation 9:1–2:

I saw a star that had fallen to the earth from the sky, and he was given the key to the shaft of the bottomless pit. When he opened it, smoke poured out as though from a huge furnace, and the sunlight and air turned dark from the smoke (NLT).

This event in Revelation 9 states clearly that the bottomless pit is in the Earth; it has an access point, and the smoke from it was literally let into the Earth's atmosphere. This is no allegory, but simple, easy- to-understand language. It may seem fantastical to some, but the Bible is clear that this is the pit that Satan is thrown into and chained up in for a thousand years.

REVELATION 20:4–6

A QUICK AND EXPEDIENT TRIAL

While Satan is bound in the pit, Jesus and the saints establish what has traditionally been called the Millennial Kingdom. They live and reign with Christ for a thousand years. I believe this ruling and judging with our delegated authority as kings and priests may be one of the first events in the Millennium. John saw *"thrones, and the people sitting on them had been given authority to judge"* (Rev. 20:4 NLT). This connects to what the apostle Paul wrote in First Corinthians 6:2–3:

> *Do you not know that the saints will judge the world? And if the world will be judged by you, are you unworthy to judge the smallest matters? Do you not know that we shall judge angels?...*

All of the saints have been with Jesus throughout the events of His triumphant return and His rescue of Jerusalem. Now it appears they are immediately put to work as Jesus establishes righteous order on the Earth. This may be the same event that Joel wrote about in Joel 3:1–2:

> *At that time of those events...when I restore the prosperity of Judah and Jerusalem, I will gather the armies of the world into the valley of Jehoshaphat. There I will judge them...* (NLT).

At the same time that this court is established, all of the martyrs from the Tribulation are also resurrected. John saw the *"the souls of those who had been beheaded for their testimony of Jesus.... They all came to life again"* (Rev. 20:4 NLT). However, *"the rest of the dead did not come back to life until the thousand years had ended"* (Rev. 20:5 NLT). If indeed the judgment of Revelation 20 is synonymous with the judgment of the Valley of Jehoshaphat, this means that those who are being judged are the *"armies of the world"* (Joel 3:2). This causes me to wonder whether the resurrected martyrs will be brought back to stand as witnesses against those who killed them.

Clearly, this thousand-year period is full of very fascinating events—some incredibly exciting and some a bit confusing. Perhaps the most mystifying part is the designation of a specific number of years. *Why is a thousand-year Kingdom necessary? And why is it just one thousand years?* I believe I have some answers.

WHY A THOUSAND-YEAR KINGDOM?

The first reason I can see for the Millennium reign of Jesus Christ is for the literal fulfillment of the myriad of promises of restoration of the people and the nation of Israel. Those promises, laced throughout Scripture, have served as inspiration for the Church to teach us how to pray and what to expect from God. We have drawn on them in faith, and the Lord has been happy to oblige. But a day will come when they will actually be fulfilled in their original context. Lands will be restored, cities will be rebuilt, borders will be enlarged, and families will be blessed. If we open our Bibles to almost anywhere in the Old Testament prophets, we will read God's promises to the Jews. They're everywhere, and many of them are not yet fulfilled. When Jesus hung on the cross, an inscription hung with Him: KING OF THE JEWS (see John 19:19). He has never yet sat as their reigning King, but He will. I want Him to. I am not threatened by that, and in no way, shape, or form does it interfere with the myriad of great and precious promises that He has for me.

When we are born into this world, we grow up in a particular context—a terrestrial habitation that is supposed to be managed by us. We are the delegated curators of this planet. We have been given freedom to alter and shape the land and the environment. I believe the Lord wanted to enjoy observing us and working with us, His children, as we discovered the nuances of this beautiful planet. He wanted us to build cities that He could marvel at. He wanted us to create sports, games, and wild and crazy activities for sheer pleasure and enjoyment. He was looking forward to extravagant theatrical productions, concerts, films, and every other kind of creative expression we could conceive.

However, God was robbed of much of that joy when our grandparents, Adam and Eve, lost dominion of the Earth. Ever since, Satan has been tirelessly at work to pervert the entire plan. When Satan succeeds at turning entertainment into pornography, art into horror, and music into death; when he succeeds at corrupting the minds of mathematicians and engineers; when he robs children of their childhood, crushing their ability to dream and imagine—He succeeds at the destruction of God's desire. He steals from God our Father the joy of watching His kids succeed, as well as the intimacy we were to have with God in worship and praise. Satan hates God; therefore, he is out to destroy that which God enjoys most—us (not just our physical beings, but our accomplishments and our dreams, too).

I believe the thousand-year Kingdom is for that exact purpose. Jesus Christ is going to get His full reward, which includes being the King of a brilliantly creative global community that accomplishes marvelous and wondrous works *on this planet and in this context* of time, space, and matter.

This conclusion begs another question: *Why wouldn't this thousand- year reign just go on forever?* For that, I have three dimensions to an overall theory.

197

First, the thousand-year Kingdom contains people who are direct descendants of those who were allowed, by God's grace, to walk directly into the Millennium. As with the rest of us, Jesus will not force them into a relationship with Him; they, too, will have to make a decision to worship Him as Lord. They, too, will have to decide to participate whole-heartedly in His plan. They will have the advantage of living under His direct physical reign, where there will be no question that He is real. However, as we will see, some (unfathomably) still choose to rebel.

The second part of my theory has to do with our relationship with the Lord. As I mentioned just prior, He still wants the pleasure of watching us create and working with us as co-creators. He wants to see what we will do with this planet, and He has chosen not to peer into that future so that He can have the joy of partnership and surprise. To this end, Proverbs 8:30-31 give us a peek into the heavenly realm, where Jesus, under the name Wisdom, is at the side of the Father as they create. Here Jesus makes a marvelous statement:

Then I was beside Him as a master craftsman; and I was daily His delight, rejoicing always before Him, rejoicing in His inhabited world, ***and my delight was with the sons of men.***

Even though Jesus has access to the heavenly realm and the processes of all the Father has, is, and does, Jesus is incomplete without us. It's like the classic scene from the movie *Jerry McGuire*, when Tom Cruise tells Rene Zellweger, "You complete me."1 Jesus wants to have fellowship with us in the context of this Earth, and He wants that more than church services and singing songs, although that is part of it. He wants the whole human interaction of digging, planting, creating, building, writing, drawing, and so forth. But that's not the end of it.

198

This leads me to the third component of my theory. After one thousand years, it will be time to move on to the next level and phase of God's plan. But we must first learn and be developed on this current Earth. Afterward, the Lord will purge creation of unbelievers once and for all, and He will conclusively deal with Satan. As amazing as this current planet is, there is more! We just can't see it from our current view. We aren't ready for infinity and beyond. The thousand-year Kingdom is for the purpose of getting us ready. In fact, I believe that, even if Adam and Eve had not fallen in the Garden, this Earth still may have expired after a certain period of time—by God's design. Of course, there would have been no death or sickness, but I believe it's possible that we could have reached a point where we had exhausted the potential of this sphere, had learned what we needed to learn, and would be introduced to a new Heaven and new Earth. This is just an idea, of course, not a theology, but I think it's a pretty good one.

KEEPING IT LITERAL

Many people struggle to embrace the concept of the Millennial Reign of Christ, and some just flat out reject the notion all together. Some say the number 1000 is God's symbol for an indefinite number or forever. That makes no sense to me at all. They have decided it is allegory, heavily relying on the often abused catch-all Bible verse found in Second Peter 3:8, *"But, beloved, do not forget this one thing, that with the Lord one day is as a thousand years, and a thousand years as one day."* They attach this verse to any long time span that they can't wrap their minds around.

But when Peter said, *"With the Lord a day is as a thousand years and a thousand years as a day,"* He was simply making a point that God is not limited by time restraints or deadlines. He can take all the time He needs to perform His will. It's the same as me saying, "I

199

don't care if it takes a week or five years; it makes no difference to me, because I am going to accomplish this goal." However, we don't want that statement to be our standard for every event in our lives. For some things, we *do* care whether it takes a week or five years. So it is with God. He has no communication problem and doesn't throw out numbers to confuse us. As a matter of good Bible interpretation practice, it is not good to take a single statement that is an obvious abstract metaphor and make it a general rule applying it out of context in other places of scripture —and then reverse the concept by taking a event that appears to be literal, real, and time sensitive and make it an allegory using a previous abstract metaphor as your basis.

The events in Revelation 20 are directly in the flow of the account of Jesus's return to the Earth. We are now in the aftermath of that grand event, and we are being given more information about what else is yet to come. This is simple reading if you let it be. This is why I prefer to read the book of Revelation like a child, believing every bit of it as true and accurate, accepting the story exactly as it reads in its simplicity. I refuse to over intellectualize this book, cutting and pasting it throughout history.

Thus, I have not allegorized much of Revelation at all. I can say with confidence that Revelation 20 and the thousand-year reign of Jesus Christ on this current Earth are not an allegory. The text reads as clear and straight as if it was history. I have read this chapter over and over, and it is one of the simplest stories in the book of Revelation (and the entire Bible) to understand. Perhaps that is the very reason why so many people struggle with it. The claims made in this chapter are simply stated, yet absolutely astonishing.

REVELATION 20:7–10

OUT ON PAROLE

At the end of these glorious thousand years, once again Satan is allowed to do his thing. As stated in verse 3, his campaign lasts just *"a little while."* To his own chagrin, he is once again easily defeated. It's like the Washington Generals against the Harlem Globetrotters. No matter how many games the Washington Generals play against the Harlem Globetrotters or how serious they are about winning, they just can't win. This is because the game results are already predetermined. Unfortunately, many people fall for Satan's deceptive plan and are destroyed in the process. Once again, it is obvious from the text that this not a battle, just as the Battle of Armageddon was never a battle. Both are one-sided victories, with Jesus the undisputed champion. Finally, Satan joins—for all eternity—the Beast and the False Prophet in the lake of fire. This is his final note in the song of history.

REVELATION 20:11–15

THE DEATH OF DEATH

Now that the destroyer is forever gone, it is time for the Final Judgment for all who have been in the grave up to that point in time. First, we need to establish who is actually in the grave. Ephesians 4:8 says, *"Therefore He says: 'When He ascended on high, He led captivity captive, and gave gifts to men.'"* From this, we can see that when Jesus was raised from the dead, graves opened up and the dead saints—all who died in faith—were resurrected. Matthew's gospel confirms this:

201

And Jesus cried out again with a loud voice, and yielded up His spirit. Then, behold, the veil of the temple was torn in two from top to bottom; and the earth quaked, and the rocks were split, and the graves were opened; and many bodies of the saints who had fallen asleep were raised; and coming out of the graves after His resurrection, they went into the holy city and appeared to many (Matthew 27:50–53).

Then, when the Rapture happens, all who have died in Christ will also be caught up with the living believers. This is made crystal clear by Paul in First Thessalonians 4:15–17:

For this we say to you by the word of the Lord, that we who are alive and remain until the coming of the Lord will by no means precede those who are asleep. For the Lord Himself will descend from heaven with a shout, with the voice of an archangel, and with the trumpet of God. And the dead in Christ will rise first. Then we who are alive and remain shall be caught up together with them in the clouds to meet the Lord in the air....

My understanding of the Rapture is that it is the main resurrection event for all believers who have died since Christ's resurrection up until that point. At the Rapture, their spirits are reunited with their bodies. Until then, dead believers exist in spirit consciousness only. But at that point, they get to put some sandals on. Then, as we have seen in this study through Revelation, Jesus will rapture new believers all the way through the Tribulation.

WHAT ABOUT THE PIGMY'S IN AFRICA?

At this juncture of the Great White Throne Judgment, the only people left are those who died in unbelief and those who died not knowing anything about God or Jesus. They will all be judged at this throne encounter. This includes those who never heard the gospel and weren't pagans or idolaters. According to verse 12, they are *"judged according to their works."* This idea may be hard to accept, but we must consider the good nature of God. He is just and fair. I personally can't imagine Him holding people accountable for information they did not know. One example would be the various indigenous people around the world who were completely disconnected from the Jewish nation or any influence or knowledge of scripture prior to the incarnation of Christ. There was no such thing as missionaries or evangelism. I suspect many mystical practices evolved due to the void of information about God. Yet they sensed Him and His presence. Romans 2:14–16 gives us some insight to this:

> *Even Gentiles, who do not have God's written law, show that they know his law when they instinctively obey it, even without having heard it. They demonstrate that God's law is written in their hearts, for their own conscience and thoughts either accuse them or tell them they are doing right. And this is the message I proclaim—that the day is coming when God, through Christ Jesus, will judge everyone's secret life* (NLT).

Thus, I believe that, at the Great White Throne Judgment, many who never heard the gospel will find their names written in the book of life. God is certainly able to apply the blood of Jesus Christ as He sees fit. He gave His own Son for them, and He will take every soul that He can without violating His Word. The rest will, unfortunately, be cast into the lake of fire with death and the grave itself.

Praise God for His incredible mercy! I look forward to the day when I will meet this new company of saints who pass through the Great White Throne Judgment. They will be a very unique group, and we will get to tell them all about Jesus and the cross and the love of God. I'm sure they will be amazed at all that was going on that they had no idea about. Praise God that we all——saints from all eras and regions, the heavenly host, and God Himself——will have all eternity to know and be known.

12. To Infinity and Beyond

REVELATION 21–22

From here on out, sin and evil will be just a memory. In one sense, we are moving forward, and in another sense, we are going back— back to the Garden. There is just one major difference; we, the inhabitants of God's new Heaven and Earth will understand the consequence and cost of unbelief. When Adam and Eve fell in the Garden, Satan's primary method of manipulation was causing them to question God's command to not eat of the tree in the middle of the Garden. He did this by posing a question, *"Has God indeed said 'You shall not eat of every tree of the garden'?"* (Gen. 3:1). Eve's first mistake was to answer him back. This conversation culminated in a lie that Eve believed, and the rest is history. Thankfully, this time Satan will be out of the picture, and there will be no more lies.

When one of my granddaughters, Josie, was eight, she was awakened in the middle of the night by a voice calling her name. She is a very spiritually discerning little girl. She didn't recognize the voice, and she didn't have a peace about it. She knew it was from the invisible realm, so she responded, "God, if that's You, keep talking. Devil, if that's you, be quite." After that, no one said anything so she went back to sleep. If only Eve had had the same discernment.

Thankfully, after the Final Judgment, all of creation will be past the influence of the lie, and we will be a company of people destined for eternity in the presence of our God. The last thousand years will have been a great learning experience and a purging process, ridding the Kingdom once and for all of rebellion. At the same time, we will have learned to be kings and priests under the direct leadership of Jesus Christ. At long last, it's time for *to infinity and beyond.* Our hearts are ready, our minds are ready, and we are anxious to move into what God has next.

REVELATION 21

THE BRIDE AND THE NEW JERUSALEM

One of the mysteries revealed in this chapter is the identity of the wife of the Lamb. As we discussed previously, the New Jerusalem is seen, in verse 2, *"coming down out of heaven from God, prepared as a bride adorned for her husband."* Then, in verses 9, an angel offers to show John *"the bride, the Lamb's wife."* He proceeds to once again show John (as if from another vantage point than verse 2) *"the great city, the holy Jerusalem, descending out of heaven from God"* (Rev. 21:10). I have already stated (in Chapter 9) that the Church-Bride, New Jerusalem-Bride relationship has always baffled me. But somehow we are in there.

Interestingly, in verse 14, we see that the foundations of the New Jerusalem have the names of the twelve apostles on them. This reminds me of what Paul wrote in Ephesians 2:20–22:

Together, we are his house, built on the foundation of the apostles and the prophets. And the cornerstone is Christ Jesus himself. We are carefully joined together in him, becoming a holy temple for the Lord. Through him you Gentiles are also being made part of this dwelling where God lives by his Spirit (NLT).

One idea I have is that we, the Church corporate joined together, create a habitation that is the body of Christ, which interacts with the New Jerusalem, which is the actual Lamb's wife. This would explain why Paul tells husbands to love their wives as they do their own bodies (see Eph. 5:23–33). Trying to separate the body of Christ, from His Bride, and His Bride from His Church is like trying to separate bone from marrow or to split the atom. It's theologically doable, just not simple.

One can only imagine the beautiful spectacle this must have been for John. According to the measurements given, the New Jerusalem is 1500 miles cubed. The following analogy gives us an idea as to the sheer size of the city compared to the Earth itself. I have heard it explained in this way: Take one stick of chewing gum, chew it up, squeeze it into a cube, and stick it to a golf ball. That's what the New Jerusalem would look like if set on this Earth. This has caused some scholars to think that this city will possibly hover over the Earth in a type of orbit, never actually touching down. Otherwise the Earth would wobble as it spins. It sounds good to me, but then again, who knows? Another possible theory is that the New Heaven and New Earth that John sees in Revelation 21:1 are much larger than the originals. That theory obviously flies in the face of the belief that the New Earth is an exact restoration of the original Earth. I personally don't think it matters. The main point, as described in verses 11–21, is the absolute magnificence and beauty of this city. It is beyond compare!

REVELATION 21:22-27

NO TEMPLE

After describing in detail the beauty of the New Jerusalem, John says, *"I saw no temple in the city, for the Lord God Almighty and the Lamb are its temple"* (Rev. 21:22 NLT). He also notes the lack of a sun and a moon. This section is self-explanatory. It's more about what's not there than what is. Some day we will worship the Lord in the fullness of His glory in our glorified bodies. The Lamb will be our temple, and the light of the Lamb will energize the entire city. Because of this, the city will be open always, and within it we will never experience night. The promises contained in these descriptions of the wife of the Lamb are almost too good to imagine, but I know they are true and that they are and will be my reality.

REVELATION 22:1–5

THE RIVER AND TREE OF LIFE

Before the end of his prophecy of the Revelation of Jesus, John is shown one last important detail of the eternal city——the river and tree of life. The river of life flows from the throne. On either side of the river (and right in the middle of the street) grows the tree of life.

Once, when I was having a house built, I told the landscape designer that I wanted a tree planted so that, from the front door, I would look through the tree out onto the street. The inspiration came from this image of the throne of God and the tree of life here in Revelation 22:1. However, the developer tried to dissuade me, saying that my design concept was bad. He said it broke the rules of fung shui, an ancient Chinese mystical design philosophy that is supposed to incorporate the laws of Heaven and Earth to improve life by facilitating positive energy. He told me the tree would keep positive energy from entering the house and disallow negative energy from leaving. I told him that I didn't care about fung shui and neither did God. The very throne of Heaven has a river that flows from it right into a tree that is in the middle of the street and on both sides. And if it's good enough for God, it's good enough for me. That tree is there today.

FRUIT OF THE MONTH CLUB

Not only does the tree grow on either side of the river, but it also bears twelve fruits and yields a crop every month of the year. I find this very interesting. It tells us that our eternal existence will be time-based. Even though life will be eternal, we will still have months or, as more accurately translated, new moons. This seems to contradict Revelation 21:23, *"And the city had no need of the sun, neither the moon, to shine in it: for the glory of God did lighten it, and the Lamb is the light thereof"* (KJV). One possible explanation for this is that the city itself is a closed ecosystem, due to the light of the Lamb, but outside the city, the world and universe still function as they do today. That makes sense to me.

John also says that *"the leaves of the tree were for the healing of the nations"* (Rev. 22:2). When I Googled this topic, I was amazed at all of the discussion it has sparked on blogs and chats. The allegories run wild, as do the heated debates. However, I did find a good website titled "12 Steps to Successful Fruit Tree Planting," so it wasn't a total loss. So here is my take on this tree:

- It's a fruit tree.

- It has twelve kinds of fruit.

- It produces a yield every month.

- Its leaves are for the healing of the nations.

Yes, I believe there is an actual tree, and it accomplishes exactly what the Bible says. People may call me a simpleton if they'd like. All I know is that if I read this to my eight-year-old granddaughter and asked her to explain it, that is what she would say.

What a simple and amazing key to eternal life—the fruit of the tree of life and its leaves, which bring healing. I can't imagine a better way to stay alive and healthy and enjoy the process. Eat fruit. I'm not kidding. Let's take it a step farther. Imagine that Jesus teaches us how to graft the tree of life in the Millennium and that we discover the ingredients and the technology were at our disposal the whole time we've been on this Earth. I bet Heaven will be full of surprises. To all the theologians who laugh at my ideas, I say this: I'm not offended. Just bake me an apple pie in Heaven, and I will forget everything you said about me.

THE LAMB'S SERVANTS

In the midst of this description of the river and tree of life, we find a reference to the 144,000 personal assistants of the Lamb of God. As we previously discussed, in Revelation 14, 12,000 Jews from each of the twelve tribes were sealed and marked on their foreheads. Here they show up again as eternal servants to the Lamb:

> *Then I saw the Lamb standing on Mount Zion, and with him were 144,000 who had his name and his Father's name written on their foreheads* (Revelation 14:1 NLT).

> *...No one could learn this song except the 144,000 who had been redeemed from the earth. They have kept themselves as pure as virgins, **following the Lamb wherever he goes.** They have been purchased from among the people on the earth as a special offering to God and to the Lamb. They have told no lies; they are without blame* (Revelation 14:3–5 NLT).

I believe that, from the events of Revelation 14:4 until now, these 144,000 may have been by Jesus's side the entire time. When He went out, they went out; when He sat on His throne, they surrounded Him with their praises. He knows them all by their secret names. And with this, the description of future events ends. All that remains are some final words from Jesus regarding what we should do as we await the end-times.

REVELATION 22:6–21

COMING QUICKLY OR QUICKLY COMING?

The focus of this book is more about general eschatology, but here I want to zero in on this statement that Jesus says three times in a very short span— *"I am coming quickly"* (Rev. 22:7,12,20). If we were reading this within a few weeks after the apostle John dictated this statement, we might think Jesus is coming at any minute. But reading this statement as we are, a couple thousand years later, we have to ask ourselves, *What was Jesus saying? Has He intended for the entire Body of Christ to believe His return could be at any moment? And if that is the case, why would He give us the book of Revelation in the first place?*

As we journeyed through Revelation, we read about incredible events on the Earth, sea, and sky. We read about entire geopolitical shifts and governmental breakdowns. We read about things that haven't happened yet. To add to the mystery, we also find in the Old Testament other large-scale events, such as Ezekiel 38, that also haven't happened yet, but that are (according to scholarly consensus) separate scenarios from the Tribulation. And then there is the prophecy I mentioned about Israel, Egypt, and Syria becoming allies before Christ returns. The borders will be open, and a single highway will connect them. And Iran will be redeemed. That is yet to happen. Considering all these factors, it's hard for me to believe Jesus intended us to believe for several thousand years that He could return tomorrow.

Rather, let me propose a theory. After examining all the times the word *quickly* (tacheos in Greek) is used in the New Testament, I have observed that it seems to be used in situations that require swift action. For example:

• When Peter's chains fell off in the jail house, the angel told him, *"Arise quickly"* (Acts 12:7).

• When Jesus sent Judas out of the last supper, He said, *"What you do, do quickly"* (John 13:27).

• The angel at the tomb of Jesus resurrection said to Mary, *"Go quickly and tell His disciples that He is risen from the dead..."* (Matthew 28:7).

Here's my point. When Jesus said that He is coming quickly and that we should be ready because the Son of Man comes at *"an hour you do not expect"* (Matt. 24:44), He was saying that when He comes it will be *swift*. This fits with what the apostle Paul said about the Rapture happening in the twinkling of an eye (see 1 Cor. 15:52). I suspect that when Jesus makes His grand return on the clouds with Heaven's armies, He will be very quick about it. But I don't believe we are supposed to assume He is coming back tomorrow and use that as a tactic to manipulate people into being good Christians. That's why we have Bible prophecy—so that we will know the season of His coming.

Many preachers today are preaching the equivalent of "Santa Claus is coming to town"—"You better watch out, you better not cry, better not pout, I'm telling you why..." In this way, the doctrine of imminent return causes pastors, theologians, preachers, and teachers to interpret every little thing that happens around the world as a sign of the times. They have to. They read the Bible and see that all these events must take place before Jesus returns, so they force fit everything in order to make their eschatology work and maintain a sense of urgency. I have been hearing it my entire life. And I can't count the number of times I have been preached at about certain events being a sign that Jesus's return is just around the corner. Every tidal wave, every war, every economic recession becomes a sign of the end.

I, however, am done with that kind of thinking. I don't know when Jesus is coming, but I do know that some day He will. When He does, it's going to happen quickly, and I plan on being ready. In fact, I'm ready right now. I'm fifty-three years old, so no matter what my eschatology, I will be seeing Him in about forty years anyway. The question is: *How am I going to spend the next four decades?* Will I warn people over and over that the end is near when, in reality, I have no idea if it is? No, I won't. I am going to show people that a loving God will heal their bodies and bless their finances. I will introduce them to a loving God who will restore their marriages and overpower them with great joy. I am going to tell the world about a hope and a future, about the guarantee that this world can be a better place with Jesus on the throne of our hearts.

I believe whole-heartedly that everything in Revelation (and the whole Bible) is true and that one day Jesus will reside as King on this planet. I believe Satan will be evicted, kicking and screaming. I believe in a brief period in history when things will appear to get worse (but, in fact, they will be getting better). I believe in all those things, but I also can clearly see that the Bible speaks of many other things that must happen beforehand. I want my children to believe they have time to raise a family, time to solve the national debt, and time to set long-term goals for missions and evangelism. I want them to live with confidence that they have time to plant new forests, go to medical or law school, and impact entire cities with the gospel. I

213

want them to even consider the idea of establishing new nations. Anything is possible. That is my vision for them. I don't want them constrained to standing on corners and yelling of doom and gloom, but I want them to be free to get involved in this world and use the anointing on their lives to lend a hand. It's time to raise more Alexanders.

END NOTES

Part 1

Introduction

1. Peter Green, *Alexander the Great and the Hellenistic Age* (Phoenix: W&N, 2007), 4.

2. Joseph Roisman and Ian Worthington, *A Companion to Ancient Macedonia* (John Wiley and Sons, 2010), 9.

Chapter 1

1. Bill Johnson, *When Heaven Invades Earth* (Shippensburg, PA: Destiny Image, 2003), 41.

2. Alexander Venter, *Doing Healing* (Cape Town, South Africa: Vineyard International Publishing, 2009), 44.

Chapter 2

1. *Blue Letter Bible,* s.v. "Perousia" (Strong's G3952).

2. On this subject, I highly recommend the books *Doing Healing,* by Alexander Venter, and *The Supernatural Power of the Transformed Mind,* by Bill Johnson.

Chapter 3

1. Josephus, *Wars Of The Jews,* Chapter IV.

2. Josephus, *Wars Of The Jews,* Chapter VI.

3. Josephus, *Wars Of The Jews I.*

4. There is some amazing film footage from inside the Dome Of The

Rock in the movie *Father of Lights* by Darren Wilson.

5. *Blue Letter Bible*, s.v. "Shiqquwts" (Strong's H8251); s.v. "Shamem" (Strong's H8074).

6. See Chuck Missler, "An Alternate Ending Part 2: Antichrist From the Middle East?" *Koininoa House*, http://www.khouse. org/articles/2002/437/#resources, and other teaching resources available at www.khouse.org. Also see Walid Shoebat's book, *Why I Left Jihad*, and other resources available at shoebat.com.

Chapter 4

1. Various videos of the glory cloud at Bethel exist on YouTube.

2. The Firestarters curriculum, written by Kevin Dedmon, isavailable at http://store.ibethel.org

Chapter 5

1. *Blue Letter Bible*, s.v. "Oikoumene" (Strong's G3625). 2. *Blue Letter Bible*, s.v. "Ge" (Strong's G1093).

Part 11

Introduction

1. *Blue Letter Bible*, s.v. "Apokalypsis" (Strong's G602).

Chapter 7

1. *Strong's Concordance*, s.v. "Aggelos" (#G32). 2. Ibid, s.v. "Cukkah" (#H5521).

Chapter 8

1. Walid Shoebat, in conversation with the author. Also see Shoetat's book, *Why I left Jihad* (New York: Top Executive Media, 2005), which explains this idea in detail, including photos from Codex

Vaticanus ancient copies of Bible manuscripts.

Chapter 9

1. Harold Eberle & Martin Trench, *Victorious Eschatology*, Second Edition (Yakima, WA: Worldcast Publishing, 2009), 188-190.

Chapter 10

1. *Blue Letter Bible,* s.v. "Apocalypto" (Strong's G601).

2. Daniel 12:11–12 speaks of a forty-five day gap that I believe is the time difference between Christ's final touchdown on Earth and the establishing of His Kingdom. This allows for the events of His return to happen in real time.

3. *Blue Letter Bible,* s.v. "Valley of Jehoshaphat" (Strong's H3092 [6]).

4. *Blue Letter Bible,* s.v. "Poieo" (Strong's G4160).

Chapter 11

1. *Jerry McGuire,* written and directed by Cameron Crow (TriStar Pictures, 1996).

GLOSSARY OF TERMS

Amillennialism—A belief that the one thousand years mentioned in Revelation 20 are symbolic of Christ's current reign on Earth that began with Pentecost via the delegated authority of the Church. This era will end with His physical and final return.

Futurism—A belief that all of the events described in the book of Revelation are yet to happen in the future.

Gematria—Hebrew numerology used to interpret Scripture by computing the numeric value of words.

Great Tribulation, the—A time prior to Christ's return when Satan and his demonic forces will be dealt with by a series of judgments from God. Also called the Day of Vengeance.

Millennium—The thousand-year reign of Christ on the Earth.
Preterism—A belief that all of the events in Scripture are historical,

including the second advent of Christ and the Final Judgment.

Partial-preterism—A belief that the events described in the book of Revelation that precede the return of Jesus in chapter 19 are historical, not future.

Pre-millennialism—A belief that Jesus will return just before the thousand-year Kingdom described in Revelation 20, thus inaugurating the thousand-year Kingdom and physically ruling on

Earth. **Post-millennialism—Very** similar to partial-preterism, with a few distinctions.

Rapture, the—Jesus coming and receiving His Church from the Earth prior to His Final Return.

18435194R00118

Made in the USA
Charleston, SC
03 April 2013